Mosley's Men in Black

Uniforms, Flags and Insignia of the
British Union of Fascists 1932-1940
& Union Movement

John Millican

Sanctuary Press Ltd

Mosley's Men in Black
Uniforms, Flags and Insignia
of the British Union of Fascists 1932-1940
& Union Movement

John Millican

Copyright © 2020 Sanctuary Press Ltd

First Edition: Brockingday Publications, London. 2004.
Second Edition: Brockingday Publications, London. 2005.
Third Edition: Sanctuary Press Limited, London. 2020.

ISBN: 978-1-912887-66-8

Sanctuary Press Ltd
71-75 Shelton Street
Covent Garden
London
WC2H 9JQ

www.sanctuarypress.com
Email: info@sanctuarypress.com

Contents

Introduction

This book is the result of many years research; it has not been an easy book to write. Unlike many of the European National Socialist Movements of the 1930's and 1940's, who published Organisation/Year books detailing their uniforms and insignia, the B.U.F. regulations concerning its uniforms were virtually restricted to internal bulletins, most of which have not survived. However, I have been fortunate in being assisted by a number of former B.U.F. members who by their excellent memories have contributed much to this study.

In 1936 the British Union of Fascists changed its name to the British Union of Fascists and National Socialists, abbreviated to British Union. However to avoid confusion I have referred to the Movement as the B.U.F. throughout the text.

It is hoped this book will be of interest to collectors and students of Sir Oswald Mosley's political Movements.

The author would welcome any additional information or corrections relating to the contents of this book.

Without the assistance of the following people this book would not have seen the light of day.

David Bale, Fred Bailey, Reg Buck, J. Elves, R.E.Hargrave, Paul Jarvis, Stuart Leeks, Roy Lewis, Eileen Mackrory, John Reynolds, E.R.Rice, Rod Roberts, Robert Row, Robert Saunders O.B.E, Jeffrey Wallder, John Warburton, Ron Webb, Stephen Western, Arthur (Archie) Wilson, and Len Wise.

I would especially like to thank Brian Molloy for his excellent artwork, which features in this book.

Last but by no means least, I would like to thank my wife Fran for her many contributions to this project, and for tolerating my sometimes obsessional approach to this subject.

John Millican

Sacrifice. Lieut. Mosley unveils the First World War
memorial in his Harrow constituency.

Sir Oswald Mosley

Sir Oswald Mosley, Leader of the British Union of Fascists, was arguably the most brilliant politician of his era. Born in 1896 into a wealthy landowning family, he was educated at Winchester School and entered the Royal Military College Sandhurst in 1913. Later that same year Mosley was gazetted at the age of 17 to the 16th Lancers, and served with them in France during the First World War. He later flew with the Royal Flying Corps on the Western Front. He was discharged from active service in 1916 due to injuries and was employed as a civil servant at the Ministry of Munitions.

Oswald Mosley,1916

Mosley went into politics with two missions in mind: to create the promised "Land Fit for Heroes to Live In" and to prevent Britain becoming involved in another Great War. He followed these two objectives throughout the remainder of his life. Mosley was elected to Parliament as Conservative M.P. for Harrow in the General Election of 1918; at the age of 22 he was the youngest member of the House of Commons. Four years later Mosley left the Conservatives, whom he considered had broken their promises to the country in general and ex-servicemen in particular, and was returned as Independent M.P. for Harrow in the 1922 General Election winning by a majority of 7,422. In 1924 he joined the Labour Party and in 1929 was appointed Chancellor of the Duchy of Lancaster in the newly elected Labour government. He was charged with finding a solution to the Unemployment problem. When the Government refused to accept his proposals, known as the Mosley Memorandum, he resigned.

Oswald Mosley leaving the New Party offices in Great George Street Westminster, to fight the election in Stoke-on-Trent. 14th October 1931.

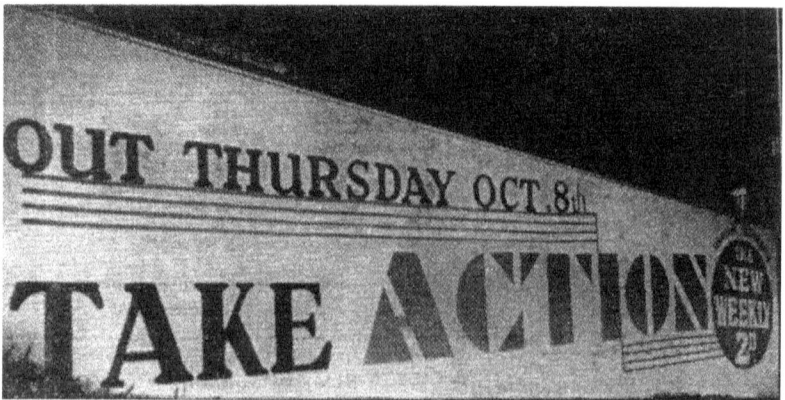

OUT THURSDAY OCT. 8th

TAKE ACTION

THE NEW WEEKLY 2d

Billboard advertisement for New Party newspaper.

The New Party

On the 1st March 1931 along with a small group of fellow M.P's he formed the New Party in an attempt to form a power base from which his radical policies could be enacted. It was ill fated from the beginning. Mosley himself fell ill with pleurisy and pneumonia, and its meetings were attacked from the start by Labourites and communists. In an attempt to obtain free speech Mosley formed a corps of stewards which became known as the 'Biff Boys'.

A few weeks after it was founded, the New Party fought a by-election at Ashton-under-Lyme and gained a respectable 4,472 votes. In the General Election of 1931 the New Party put up 24 candidates but fared badly and the party was soon dissolved.

In January 1932 Mosley visited Italy to observe Mussolini's Fascist state first hand. Immensely impressed with the economic reforms and the country's new self respect under the Fascist government, he resolved to form a Fascist Movement in Britain.

Hold high the Marigold! 'New Party' lapel badge.

Sir Oswald Mosley in B.U.F. uniform.

The British Union of Fascists

On October 1st 1932 Sir Oswald Mosley published '*The Greater Britain*' in which he set out a blueprint for a Fascist Britain. Mosley advocated a vigorous radical programme including the Occupational Franchise. Under this system Parliament would be elected not by geographical constituencies but by vocational corporations consisting of managers and workers. Other important aspects of Mosley's programme were the revival of British agriculture, military preparedness and a huge public works scheme that would systematically replace the slums and provide work for the unemployed. His new Movement would be intensely nationalistic and could be summarised by such slogans as 'Britain First' and 'Britain for the British'.

On the 3rd October 1932 the British Union of Fascists was officially launched by 32 founder members. Mosley was joined in his epic struggle, not only by some of the more robust of his New Party supporters many of whom were from the uniformed NUPA (New Party Youth Movement), but also by former members of the small British Fascist groups which had existed since the early 1920's. Members of one such group, the British National Fascisti, supplied the backbone of the B.U.F's newly formed Fascist Defence Force.

In February 1933 *The Blackshirt* was published as the official newspaper of the Movement - initially a monthly publication it soon become a weekly. It claimed by 1934 to have the highest circulation of any political weekly.

No. 25. OCT. 14th—OCT. 20th, 1933   **"BRITAIN FIRST"**   ONE PENNY

Masthead of *The Blackshirt* the original B.U.F. newspaper.

All active male members wore the famous Black shirt uniform. Women members recruited for the first time in March 1933 also wore a uniform, and were organised in a separate formation under women officers. The B.U.F. quickly established a network of over

First Fascist march through London, July 11th 1933.

350 branches throughout Great Britain. Organisation was on quasi-military lines: each branch consisted of 'Units' under the charge of a Branch Organiser who was in turn under the supervision of an Inspecting Officer.

The Movement immediately began a propaganda campaign with a series of marches and meetings up and down the country. Many meetings were held on street corners but others where Mosley spoke were major Blackshirt rallies. In the early days Mosley addressed large audiences at Trafalgar Square, the Royal Albert Hall (four

Oswald Mosley speaks at the Royal Albert Hall, 1935.

meetings), Olympia and Hyde Park: the last two events being the subject of organised violence from Communist Party militants and other extreme left activists.

In the autumn of 1933 the B.U.F. moved its National Head Quarters to a former teachers training college next to the Duke of York barracks in the Kings Road, Chelsea. The new headquarters became known as the Black House and it contained extensive offices, dormitories, gym, dining hall, mess room and parade ground. Also based at Black House was the 'I' Squad - the full time mobile defence force commanded by Eric Hamilton Piercy.

Silver Jubilee 1935 - King George and Queen Mary drive past the Black House on the Kings Road, Chelsea and are enthusiastically greeted with the Fascist salute, *The Blackshirt* June 14, 1935

By early 1934 the B.U.F. membership had risen to over 50,000, many of these members joining through the publicity given to the Movement by the *Daily Mail*. This support was short lived as the owners of the paper and many new members did not understand the true nature of the B.U.F. believing it to be some sort of right-wing conservative group.

By late 1935 the B.U.F. had become a mass movement in East London, where it campaigned against the problems aggravated by the influx of 150,000 East European immigrants in an area which already suffered from serious housing shortages, high unemployment and widespread poverty. It is said Mosley developed a rapport with the people of East London which was unique in British politics. The B.U.F. abstained from the 1935 General Election having had insufficient time to develop its electoral machine. It strongly supported Edward VIII who the B.U.F. saw as an ideal Fascist monarch and during the Abdication crisis it ran a vigorous 'Stand by the King' campaign.

BUF HQ at Black House, Kings Road, Chelsea. 1934.

In early 1935 the B.U.F. underwent extensive reorganisation in which the Movement was structured on more conventional party political lines. Local districts were based on parliamentary constituencies. The membership was divided into three divisions, with the First and Second Division members being organised into Units. The most committed members in Division One were permitted to wear the uniform previously worn by the now disbanded 'I' Squad. Division Two members wore the ordinary Blackshirt uniform and Division Three members were non-uniformed. In the changes Neil Francis-Hawkins became Director of Blackshirt Organisation and in January

1936 Director-General of Organisation - the Number Two position in the Movement. In June 1935 the B.U.F. moved from their Black House N.H.Q. to offices at Sanctuary Buildings in Great Smith Street, Westminster. These were retained until the Movement was banned in 1940. The B.U.F. launched a new weekly newspaper *Action* in February 1936. In conjunction with this a new uniform was made available to active B.U.F. members who sold a certain number of copies of the paper. The new uniform called the 'Action Press' uniform was semi-military in appearance, and was said to be based on the uniform of the Brigade of Guards.

BUF parade in the grounds of Black House, Chelsea.

On Sunday October 4th 1936 serious rioting by communists prevented a march by 7,000 Blackshirts through East London to mark the fourth anniversary of the founding of the B.U.F. It had planned to assemble at Royal Mint Street, Tower Hill for inspection by Mosley and then march through East London to meetings in four B.U.F. strongholds. The disturbances became known as the 'Battle of Cable Street'. The most serious violence occurred when police moved in to remove obstructions blocking Cable Street and were attacked by left-wing thugs. This and associated violence against the B.U.F. was later used by the Government as a pretext to ban political uniforms in 1937.

The disturbances had the effect of increasing support for Mosley in East London; many ordinary people disgusted by the Red violence threw their support behind the B.U.F. Ten days after the 'Battle of

Cable Street' Mosley held a huge meeting in Limehouse, after leading an impromptu march from Bethnal Green which was another B.U.F. stronghold. This proved beyond doubt the tremendous support the Movement had in East London. In March 1937 the B.U.F. fought the London County Council elections in East London and scored remarkable votes for such a new Movement. These elections showed once again the level of support *The Blackshirts* enjoyed in East London with votes of up to 24% in some areas.

Mosley speaks to a huge crowd of supporters at Ridley Road, Dalston. 1939.

The passing of the Public Order Act 1936, which made the wearing of political uniforms illegal from January 1st 1937, was primary aimed at the B.U.F. It is worth noting however that the B.U.F. was by no means the only uniformed political organisation: amongst the many other uniformed groups were the Social Credit Greenshirts. Also much in evidence were the red shirted Independent Labour Party and the khaki clad Young Communists. To avoid possible censure from the act, the B.U.F. de-militarised its organisation: for example the London Command became London Administration and District Officers would in future be known as District Leaders.

Although banned from marching through their principal stronghold of East London, the Movement did however stage a series of spectacular marches in other areas of London from 1937 onwards. Major marches

Raven Thomson speaking at Victoria Park Square, Bethnal Green, 5th May 1940.

were held from Kentish Town to Trafalgar Square (July 1937); Westminster to Bermondsey (October 1937 and May 1938); and from the Embankment to Ridley Road, Dalston, in May 1939 where Mosley's speech was heard by an estimated crowd of over 100,000.

In July 1939 the B.U.F. held what was at that time the largest indoor meeting ever held in the world, when Mosley spoke to an audience of 30,000 at a huge Peace Rally at Earls Court. This meeting took place without any interruption whatsoever.

After war was declared in September 1939, the B.U.F. continued to campaign for 'Peace with Honour', but in May 1940 Mosley was arrested and detained under the infamous Defence Regulation 18b for his peace activities. Soon over 1,000 of his supporters followed him into prison, and the Government moved quickly to smash the B.U.F. as an organisation. With the destruction of the B.U.F. Britain's last chance for a peaceful conclusion to the war disappeared.

Mosley supporters July 1938

Emblems of the British Union of Fascists

The Fasces

From its foundation in October 1932 the B.U.F. adopted the symbol of Imperial Roman Authority, the Fasces, as its emblem. It stated that the bundle of sticks symbolised the strength of unity: divided they may be broken, united they are invincible. The axe symbolised the supreme authority of the organised state, to which every section and faction owes allegiance.[1] Although the Fasces was first used in modern times by Mussolini, the B.U.F. argued that their right to use this emblem was based on the fact that the British Empire had become chief custodian of the Roman tradition of civilisation, and the Fasces had been use in Britain since Roman times.

Examples of the fasces emblem in use between 1932 - 1936.

In March 1934 the official badge of the Movement changed from being a simple gold Fasces to a Union Flag shield with the Fasces mounted upon it. Two reasons were given for the change. Firstly, as the Movement was a patriotic body loyal to the King and Country it had been considered desirable to link the National emblem with the Fascist emblem, and secondly it had become necessary to have a badge easily distinguishable in foreign countries as a sign of the

---

1   *The Greater Britain*, Oswald Mosley. 1932.

British Blackshirts.[2] The Fasces was featured on B.U.F. printed propaganda, and on badges, flags and other items. Some examples of the various types of Fasces in use are shown, these were used between the years 1932 and 1936

The red, white and blue 'Flash & Circle' emblem.

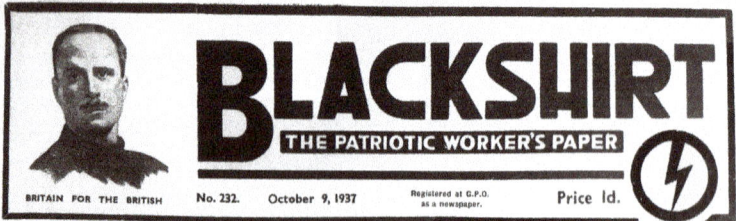

BLACKSHIRT
THE PATRIOTIC WORKER'S PAPER

BRITAIN FOR THE BRITISH   No. 232.   October 9, 1937   Registered at G.P.O. as a newspaper.   Price Id.

THROUGH PERIL TO VICTORY !

The 'Flash and Circle' used on the masthead of 'The Blackshirt'.

2   *The Fascist Week*. March 9th-15th 1934.

The Flash and Circle

Although the Fasces continued to be used throughout the 1930's by the B.U.F., its importance diminished from the summer of 1935, when a new emblem, the Flash and Circle was introduced. This gradually superseded the Fasces. The new emblem was said to represent the flash of action within a circle of unity.

According to Sir Oswald Mosley, Eric Hamilton Piercy, the Commander of the Fascist Defence Force, designed the emblem. The official colours were, a white Flash and Circle on a blue roundel with a red background. Shown below are some of the types of Flash and Circle used, including the original short lived inverted emblem, which was used briefly in 1935. The others were employed at various times between 1935 and 1940.

FASCIST HEADQUARTERS BULLETIN

Q. M. STORES. Uniforms are drawn from this department, Branch Members applying through their Organiser. The Undress Shirt is worn for the first two months of service, at the expiration of this probationary period the Full Dress may be worn.

Prices:
```
        Undress Shirt..............3/3d.
        Undress Shirt, Flannel......7/6d.
        Full Dress Shirt & Sash.....7/6d.
        Uniform trousers........8/6d. & 14/-
        Black shoes.............9/-  & 10/9
        Black boots.................8/6d.
```
The cost of these may be spread over a period by arrangement with the Q.M.Stores. Membership Cards must be produced when drawing stores.

Fascist Headquarters Bulletin, November 1933.

Three generations of Blackshirts, 1933.

Uniforms of the British Union of Fascists

The Early Years 1932 – 1933

From the earliest days of the B.U.F., its active male members wore as a uniform the famous Black shirt, modelled on Sir Oswald Mosley's fencing tunic. Mosley stated that the Black shirt was worn because the colour black best expressed the iron determination of Fascism in the face of red anarchy.[3] Apart from the obvious advantage of enabling Blackshirts to recognise each other, and act as a disciplined body while defending their meetings from attack, it was also said that by eliminating distinctions of dress it contributed to the breaking down of class barriers within the Movement.

The Black shirt was actually a close fitting, fencing style jacket, with a high polo neck, and was fastened from the neck down the left side with buttons. Although most were made from cotton, various other materials were used, including silk and velvet.

The Black shirt tunic worn by male members of the B.U.F. from the foundation of the Movement in 1932, until the banning of political uniforms under the Public Order Act 1936. These tunics were made out of a wide range of materials, from silk to velvet, and secured by ten buttons down the left side. The tunics were worn for practical as well as ideological reasons; in street fights the tunic had little an opponent could get a grip on.

---

3 *Fascism,* Oswald Mosley. 1936.

Photograph of a young member of the B.U.F. c.1933.

Blackshirts marching in 1933. Many Blackshirts still wore grey trousers.

Originally a cummerbund was worn with the Black shirt. This was replaced from the summer of 1933 with a wide black leather belt, with a large nickel-plated buckle on which was mounted a silver Fasces badge. In the very early days, regulations stipulated that grey flannel trousers should be worn with the uniform, later black trousers were substituted.[4]

Union Jack cloth tunic badge.

Example of gilt wire Fasces, worn by officers on the tunic in place of the usual brass badge, 1933-1935.

Fasces emblem on belt buckle.

From the autumn of 1932 until the spring of 1933, probationary Blackshirts wore the Grey shirt, it had patch pockets and black shoulder straps, and was worn with a black tie, cummerbund and grey trousers. This was very similar to the later Youth Movement uniform. By mid 1933, probationary members were wearing the

4   *We Marched with Mosley*. R.R.Bellamy. Black House Publishing, 2013

Blackshirt uniform belt and buckle being worn in 1934.
This was introduced in late 1933 for wear with full uniform.

Blackshirts parade in late 1933.

Blackshirts parade before entraining to Manchester early 1933.
Note probationary Blackshirts wearing the Grey uniform.

undress Black shirt, with collar and tie, for the first two months of membership, after which they were permitted to wear the full Dress uniform.

A small brass (officially described as gold) Fasces badge had been worn on the left breast of the Black shirt from 1932; this was replaced in December 1933 with a small cloth Union Flag.[5] The change was to give the Movement a more British appearance, complaints had been voiced in the Fascist press by members living abroad who had been mistaken for Italian fascists when in uniform. However by early 1934 the Union Flag had been dropped, and many fascists reverted to (or perhaps continued) wearing the original Fasces badge. Throughout the entire period that uniforms were worn, Sir Oswald Mosley wore his with no insignia whatsoever.

---

5   B.U.F. Headquarters Bulletin. December 9th 1933.

'I' Squad. 1934

The 'I' Squad

The No.1 Division, N.H.Q. were based at Black House, the B.U.F. Chelsea N.H.Q., and were better known as the 'I' Squad. This was the full time Fascist Defence Force formed in 1933 and commanded by Eric Hamilton Piercy. The 'I' Squad was divided into four units of nine men,[6] and one of its main functions was to act as escort to Sir Oswald Mosley, other duties included guarding the Black House complex and rescuing Blackshirt speakers from violent opponents. They were distinguished from ordinary Blackshirt's by wearing black breeches and black leather knee boots (many wore ex-British Army field boots), in place of the usual black trousers and shoes. On the left breast of their tunics members wore a silver badge in the form of a figure one. The 'I' Squad disappeared with the re-organisation of the Movement in 1935.

'I Squad' member 1934.

---

6   *Mosley's Blackshirts*. Arthur Beavan chapter. Edited by Len Wise. 1986.

```
QUARTERMASTERS STORES, B.U.F.

MADEIRA HALL: MADEIRA RD: STREATHAM.S.W.16.
                PRICE LIST.

BADGES.                              Price.  Post Free
Enamel........(Branches 6d each.)     9d
Badges of Rank..Flashes 6d Bars..    1d each
Cloth Badges.(Gilt Wire).........     9d
Motifs for Bathing costumes etc..     6d
BATHING COSTUMES.
Best quality.(see footnote).Prom..7/6d
BELTS.
Fascists........................     1/6d ... 1/8
Officers........................     5/6d        5/-
Womens..........................     1/6d
BRASS WARE (with Fasces emblem)
Ash Trays.......................     1/-
Bells...........................     1/9d
Brushes.........................     2/3d
Forks...........................     1/3d
Knockers........................     1/6d
Pokers..........................     1/3d
BLOUSES. (Womens Uniform)
1st quality (with tie)..........     4/9d
2nd quality ....................     3/-
CAPS.
Uniform type....................     4/6d
Black leatherette.(Ski Pattern)..    2/-
COATS
Black Uniform...................    20/-           21/-
Blk: Lthrtte,Comp:Flce Lnd.....17/6d
  "    "  Heavier Qual,D.B.&Belt.21/
CUFF LINKS
Fascist,Enamel.(Torpedo & Badge).   2/-
DOLLS
Blackshirt Dolls................    2/6d
JACKETS.
Black Macinaw Lumber Jackets.....11/6d

NOTEPAPER. (Headed)                  Price. Post
For use of Branches only.........   1/- per 10
PENCILS
Pencils with Fasces etc(Branches 1d)  1½d
PENNANTS.(Fascist)
Cycle.Complete with staff...........  9d
Moter Cycle "    "    " ............2/6d
Car       "    "    " ............3/-
PULLOVERS.
Black woollen.Roll Collar.........  2/3d
2nd quality ditto................  5/6d
1st.quality ditto................  7/6d.
SHOES.
Black Oxford,Leather sole.Med.toe..10/-
SHIRTS.
Uniform 1st.qual:................... 7/6d    6/1
    "    2nd.qual:................  5/6d
Blk.Undress spl:qual.Polo Collar... 3/3d
Do:Flannel............"....,".....  3/6d
Do.Sateen.Pocket.Zipp.."    "  ...  3/11d
Do:Poplin.Pocket.....  "    "  ...  4/6d
Do.Tunic.2 collars.T.T.& S.......  5/6d
Blk.Sprts: short slves.B.U.F.Motif. 3/-    ...3
SKIRTS.
Grey Flannel.....................10/6d
TIES.
Black............................   9d
Fascist (Black with flash)........ 2/6d
TROUSERS
Uniform..........................  8/6d
Ditto.Spl.line while stock lasts... 4/6d
BATHING COSTUMES ARE MANUFACTURED BY THE BEST
PRICES AND PARTICULARS ON APPLICATION.
(Signed) R.Nelson. Quartermaster,B.U.F.
All orders to be sent with cash to:- B.U.F.
GREAT SMITH STREET, WESTMINSTER S.W.1.
```

Quarter-masters Stores Price List 1935.

Oswald Mosley addresses public meeting in Manchester, 1933.

The Mass Movement 1934 – 1936

By early 1934 the B.U.F. membership had grown to an estimated 50,000 members, and uniformed Blackshirts were a common sight in cities and towns throughout the country.

With the B.U.F's expansion in Scotland during 1934, a new innovation peculiar to Scotland was introduced. This was a special B.U.F. kilt which was worn with the Black shirt. The colour was described as a neutral grey. Tartan being unsuitable as Fascist policy was to embrace all clans and classes.[7]

During 1934 and 1935 there were experiments with various types of uniform head wear. For a time in the summer of 1935 peaked caps were worn, bearing either a gilt Fasces badge or one featuring a Union Flag on which was mounted a gilt Fasces.

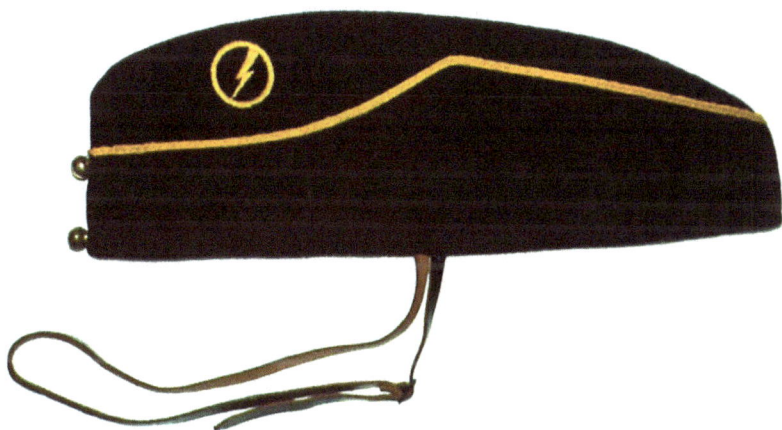

The BUF uniform forage cap 1935.

In November 1935 it was officially announced that the forage cap would in future be the only head wear permitted, and could only be worn in full dress uniform, however the wearing of the cap was not compulsory.[8] It was a black side cap, piped in yellow, with an embroidered yellow Flash and Circle to one side. To the front were two gilt droplets, and it had a black patent leather chinstrap.

7   *The Blackshirt.* January 12th-18th 1934.

8   *The Blackshirt.* November 29th 1935.

The uniform forage cap did not prove popular and had virtually disappeared by early 1936 when the new 'Action Press' uniform became available to active members. The forage cap was later revived in July 1936 for wear by the cadets, and by 1939 was being worn by the Movement's band as at the Earls Court Rally in July 1939.

The B.U.F. underwent reorganisation in early 1935, the membership now being placed into three divisions. One minor uniform change emanating from this was that members holding First Division membership (initially in a Unit giving five nights a week service to the Movement, later reduced to two nights), were permitted to wear the uniform formerly worn by the now disbanded 'I' Squad. This consisted of black breeches and leather boots, which were worn with the regulation Black shirt. In May 1936 the B.U.F. published a new 'Constitution and Regulations',[9] which gave details of the Movements uniform dress regulations; many of these had in fact been in force since re-organisation in May 1935. The black and yellow lanyard mentioned

Members of the Transport Section pose with one of their vans, 1935.
The drivers are wearing the short lived peaked caps.

---

9   British Union Constitution and Regulations. May 1936.

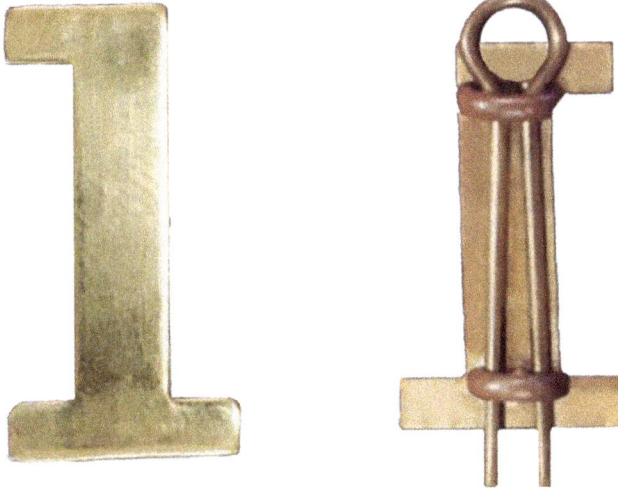

Brass Division One badge.

in the new regulations, do not appear to have been worn. The brass First Division numeral 1 was worn from 1936 but was not worn as stated on the right chest of the tunic. Shortly after the 'Constitution and Regulations' were published in May 1936 an appendix was issued in which revised instructions concerning the wearing of the First Division badge were given: it stated that the badge should be worn on the left breast.

In the British Union 'National Routine Orders' of July 13th 1936, the following details are given: "Brass numeral "1" will be worn on the left breast below medal ribbons and badges of rank. Brass numerals not to be worn on 'Action Press' uniform'.[10] The appendix also mentioned that a brassard would be added to the First Division uniform. This was later also worn by Second Division members, although it does not seem to have been compulsory for either divisions.

The B.U. 'National Routine Orders' gives details on how the brassard should be worn: "Brassards are worn on the left arm, the top edge being 8½" below the point of the shoulder". The brassard was a red cotton armband on which was an embroidered badge, featuring a white Flash and Circle on a blue roundel.

---

10   British Union National Routine Orders by the Director-General of Organisation. Serial No 316-325 Dress. July 13th 1936.

B.U.F. uniform brassard.

As the financial cost of acquiring a uniform meant many poorer members were unable to fully outfit themselves, the B.U.F. attempted to address the problem. In October 1935,[11] a reward scheme was introduced to encourage members to sell greater numbers of the B.U.F. newspaper *The Blackshirt*. This enabled members to equip themselves at no cost with the Movement's full uniform. A Blackshirt selling, for example, 320 copies of the paper in a 4-week period would earn a uniform shirt or belt. Other uniform items could be awarded for higher sales, these included boots, breeches, greatcoat and mackintosh. This scheme also applied to women members.

In the late 1934 to early 1935 period, several B.U.F. Branch Defence Forces (soon to disappear with re-organisation) introduced special badges to be awarded to members for efficiency. For example in Leeds, 26 members of the branch's Defence Force were presented in January 1935 with a special badge for smartness and efficiency.[12] This embroidered cloth badge consisted of a Fasces above which were the letters D.F.Y. (presumably Defence Force Yorkshire); the badge was worn on the left breast of the Black shirt. These badges seem to have been official but produced on local initiative and the design differed from branch to branch. Members of Battersea Branch Defence Force, for instance, wore a badge with the letters D.F.L. (Defence Force London?) below the Fasces badge. Even as late as 1936 some Blackshirt's continued to wear the old Fasces badge on their uniforms.

---

11   *The Blackshirt*. October 14th 1935.

12   *The Blackshirt*. January 4th 1935.

Drawing of the special cloth badge awarded to members of the Leeds Defence Force in January 1935. The badge was worn on the left breast of the uniform tunic.

An internal 'Quarter Masters Stores' sales list for late 1935 had officers gilt wire Fasces badges for sale, so they were presumably still being worn, but not the gilt metal Fasces badges which had obviously been phased out. Most Blackshirts at this time wore no insignia on the uniforms.

There are several badges that were used briefly during the 1934 – 1936 period that should be mentioned. Members of the Transport Section originally wore an embroidered cloth badge in the form of a gold wheel on the right sleeve of their Black shirt, however this would seem to have been very short lived.

The Movement's band also at various times sported special badges: in early 1934 it was proposed that bandsmen should wear an embroidered badge featuring a drum. However there is no photographic evidence that this was actually worn.

Bugle badge as worn by buglers. c.1936

A badge that was definitely worn by the Movement's buglers was in the form of crossed bugles, this was worn on the upper left arm of the Black shirt, the colour is unknown. This badge again had a brief existence; it was certainly in use in early 1936 at the Albert Hall rally of March 1936, but not seen thereafter.

A Blackshirt wearing an 'Action Press' style brassard. These brassards were of the same manufacture as those worn with the 'Action Press' uniform, however, the red cloth band worn on the AP uniform was wider. Interestingly it shows that even as late as 1936 some Blackshirts were still wearing the gilt Fasces badge on their tunics.

Style of brassard worn with the 'Action Press' uniform.

A Blackshirt wearing a Defence Force London cloth badge, also of interest in this late 1934 picture is a member wearing a peaked cap with metal shield badge.

Section VIII - Dress [13]

1. The Black Shirt

(169)   Members: Personal Appearance

All members must realise that the growth of the Movement depends not only on its doctrines but also on their personal appearance. It is therefore their duty, whether in uniform or plain clothes, to dress neatly. First division members who act as agents for Action Press Ltd., may wear the approved uniform of that Company.

(170)   Regulation Dress

The approved uniforms of the Movement are as follows:-

(i) First Division members who do not act as agents for Action Press Ltd., will wear the full-dress black shirt, belt, black trousers or black breeches and black field boots, black and yellow lanyard on right shoulder and numeral 1 on the right of the chest.

(ii) Second Division members will wear full-dress Blackshirt with belt, trousers and black shoes.

(iii) Third Division members may wear a black shirt with collar and black tie with plain clothes. They may be purchased from Abbey Supplies Ltd. or any clothier, but will not in any sense be provided by the Movement. This undress black shirt may also be worn by members of (I) or (II) Division when not in uniform.

(iv) Division I and II Members may wear a black double breasted uniform greatcoat over their uniform.

(171)   Women's Uniform

First Division members who act as agents for Action Press Ltd., may wear the uniform of the Company.

First Division members who do not act as agents for

---

13   Uniform details as given in the British Union Constitution & Regulations, May 1936.

Action Press Ltd., will wear the black fencing tunic without armlet or distinguishing badges. Second Division members will wear the undress black shirt with black tie.

(172) Third Division members will wear the British Union badge with plain clothes. The wearing of the black shirt is not compulsory and is to be regarded as a privilege. It is not worn by any member during the probationary period.

(173) Issue of Uniforms

All uniform other than uniform issued by Action Press Ltd or the undress black shirt, will be obtained against payment on application to Abbey Supplies Ltd., on the written authority of the D.O..

(174) Improper Dress

In no circumstances will a member introduce or wear any uniform which is not of regulation pattern, neither will he wear any article of clothing purporting to be an adequate substitute for the approved pattern.

(175) Occasions for wearing the Uniform

Members may not, without special permission from their D.O. take part in the activities of other organisations whilst in uniform.

(176) Members will not attend any Court of Law, whether as principals, witnesses or spectators in full or undress black shirts.

(177) Uniform will be worn at meetings, on marches and on occasions when any forms of ceremonial are observed.

2. Medals And Badges

(178) Medals and orders will only be worn with uniform on such occasions as may be directed by N.H.Q., viz. Mass demonstrations, Armistice Day, etc.. At all other times ribbons only will be worn. All badges authorised will be obtained against payment on application to Abbey Supplies Ltd.

Abbey Supplies despatch department.

Abbey Supplies receipt for uniform items, September 1936.

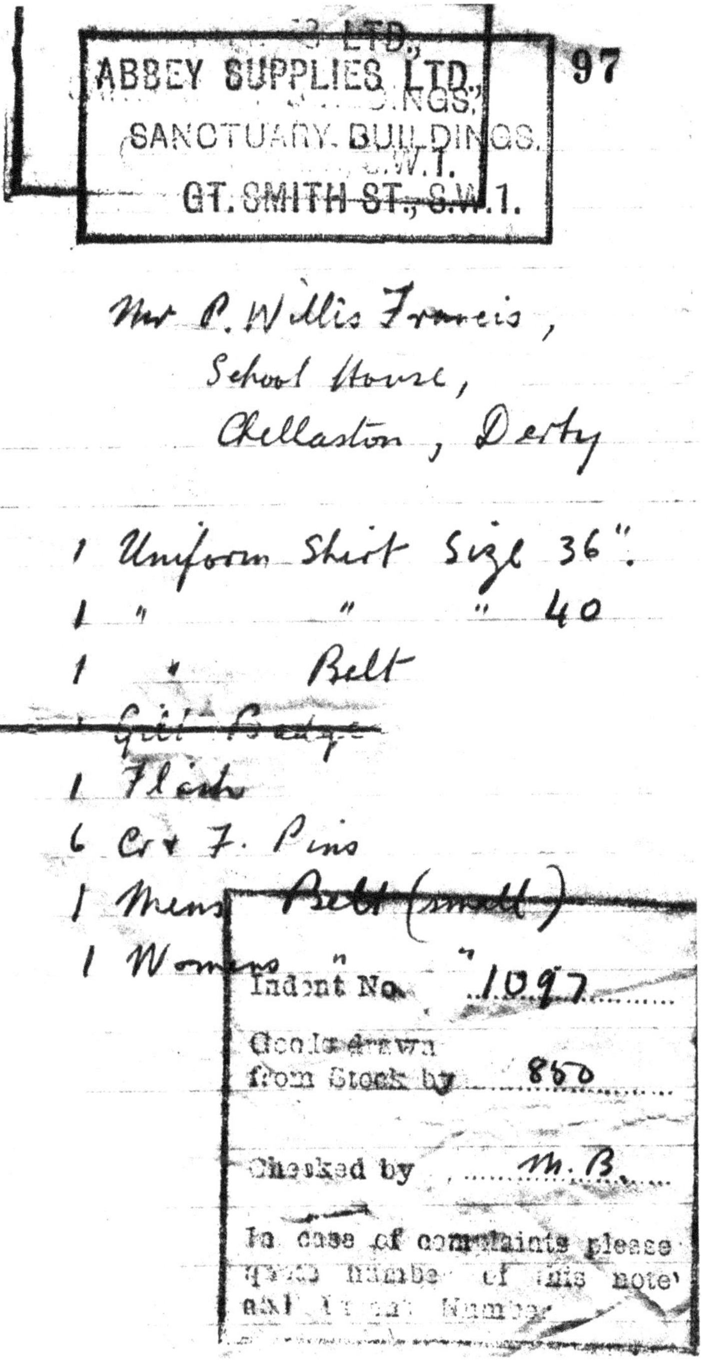

ABBEY SUPPLIES LTD. **97**
SANCTUARY BUILDINGS,
GT. SMITH ST., S.W.1.

Mr P. Willis Francis,
School House,
Chellaston, Derby

1 Uniform Shirt Size 36".
1 " " " 40
1 " Belt
~~1 Girl Badge~~
1 Flash
6 Cr & F. Pins
1 Mens Belt (small)
1 Womens " "

Indent No. 1097
Goods drawn
from Stock by 880

Checked by M.B.

In case of complaints please
quote number of this note
and Indent Number.

Abbey Supplies receipt for uniform items, September 1936.

Oswald Mosley with women members of the B.U.F. June 1934.

Marjorie Aitken leads the Women's Defence Corps 1934.

The Women's Uniform 1933 – 1936

Women played an important role in the B.U.F., and participated fully in all the Movement's activities. By the mid 1930's they made up perhaps as much as one third of the membership. Sir Oswald Mosley stated in 1940 that "My Movement was largely built up by the fanaticism of women; they hold ideals with a tremendous passion, without women. I could not have got a quarter of the way".

A woman's B.U.F. uniform 1934.

As a result of controversy over the style of the black shirts worn by women members at the Royal Albert Hall rally in April 1934, the regulations relating to women's uniforms at that time were spelt out in 'The Woman Fascist'.[14] It stated that "full uniform for B.U.F. Women's Section consists of a plain Black shirt", (actually a blouse with two patch pockets), "and tie, as issued by W.H.Q...the new "flash" ties are not permitted, a grey or black skirt, dark stockings and low heeled shoes. Black berets

14   *The Woman Fascist*. No 5 April 26th 1934.

Three female members of the B.U.F. in uniform 1934.

may be worn, but women stewards should appear bare headed". Although not mentioned a brass Fasces badge was worn on the tie.

In August 1934 a uniform belt was introduced to complete the women's uniform. It was a narrow black leather belt with nickel clasps embossed with the Fasces, and was priced at 1/6d each or 17/- a dozen.[15]

A 'Women's Defence Corps' (also referred to as the Women's Defence Force) was formed in early 1934 by six women members and was based at Black House, from this nucleus grew the women's 'Special Propaganda Section'.[16] Although both groups operated simultaneously for a period with members serving in both, the S.P.S. eventually took over the functions of the W.D.C. The S.P.S. conducted both indoor and outdoor meetings all over London held by their own speakers and stewarded by members. The women were organised in units of six giving five nights a week service to the Movement.[17] This special group was permitted to wear the Black shirt tunic as worn by the men,

15   *The Woman Fascist.* No 12 August 2nd 1934.

16   *The Blackshirt.* May 3rd 1935.

17   Memorandum on Re-organisation. May 22nd 1935.

on the left breast of their uniform was worn an embroidered badge of a Fasces under which were the letters 'S.P.S.'. The colour was probably gold. The 'Special Propaganda Section' was disbanded with the re-organisation of the Movement in May 1935.

Other badges worn in this period should be mentioned. In 1934 some women were wearing an oblong badge bearing the letters W.S. with a bar through the initials, above the pocket on the left breast of their blouse: the letters presumably stood for Women's Section. The reason for this short-lived badge is not known. A new badge of gilt Fasces mounted on a Union Flag shield replaced the original Fasces badge in March 1934, this the women wore on their uniform tie and beret.

As previously mentioned the B.U.F. introduced a new scheme in October 1935 to encourage members to sell greater numbers the their newspaper *The Blackshirt*. As a reward for increased sales women members were rewarded prizes in the same way as men. For instance, a woman selling three hundred and twenty copies of *The Blackshirt* within four weeks was rewarded with a uniform blouse and belt. If she sold six hundred and forty copies within eight weeks she was entitled to a uniform skirt.[18]

Woman's blouse badge.

---

18   *The Blackshirt.* October 14th 1935.

Blackshirt S.P.S. woman officer, 1935.

John Sant inspects women B.U.F. members, Bradford 1935.
Note the mixture of uniforms worn at this time.

The 'British Union Constitution and Regulations' published in May 1936 gives details of the women's uniform, these differed little from those in force from May 1935. Initially First Division women members operated under similar conditions of service as the former S.P.S. (giving five nights service a week to the Movement, later reduced to two nights), and were entitled to wear the black fencing tunic. During 1936 a brass numeral 1 was added to the men's First Division uniform, however women were not permitted to wear this badge. Second Division members wore the undress Black shirt (blouse) with a black tie.[19]

---

19   British Union Constitution and Regulations. May 1936.

Member of the B.U.F. in Action Press uniform. It should be noted that this
Blackshirt has added an "unofficial" button to his tunic.

The 'Action Press' Uniform

In conjunction with the launch of the B.U.F. newspaper *Action*, in February 1936, a completely new uniform was introduced to encourage members to sell the Movement's papers. The 'Action Press' uniform as it was called was supplied by Action Press Limited. This was a B.U.F. controlled company that published *Action*, and for a short period *The Blackshirt*. The uniform was officially the company livery to be worn by its selling agents; there were versions of the uniform for both men and women.

To qualify for a uniform under the 'Action Press' uniform scheme a B.U.F. member had to meet all the following conditions: -

• To hold B.U.F. Division One membership.

• Sell 13 copies of the 2d *Action* per week. (Until the end of April 1936 sales of *The Blackshirt* were included in this scheme. 26 copies of *The Blackshirt* at 1d had to be sold per week).

• To serve one months probation as an agent for 'Action Press Limited'.

Once these conditions had been met a member could then purchase their uniform at two thirds of cost price. There was also an arrangement whereby the uniform could be bought in instalments. Initially the uniform had been supplied free of charge but this was discontinued for financial reasons. If the contract was broken (i.e. the quota of papers not sold) the uniform was withdrawn. It was stated by 'Action Press Limited' that Sir Oswald Mosley sold his quota of papers.[20] One restriction the B.U.F. placed on the use of this uniform was that (for obvious reasons) it should not be worn for stewarding duties; instead the normal Division One uniform was to be worn.[21]

As many as 500 B.U.F. members may possibly have worn the 'Action Press' uniform in the February to December 1936 period. As with many other aspects concerning the B.U.F. uniforms, the shortage of documentation only makes it possible to reach general assumptions. In this case we have relied solely on the recollections of former members.

---

20   'Yorkshire Post'. January 28th 1937.

21   Letter from Lt. Col. C.S. Sharpe. Assistant Director-General of Organisation (G). May 20th 1936.

A former member of the North East Bethnal Green Branch recollects that approximately 20 members wore the 'Action Press' uniform out of the branch's 150 uniformed members; he declined to wear the uniform himself as he considered it 'too German'. This branch in 1936 was one of the largest in the B.U.F's East London stronghold.[22]

A one-time Leeds branch official who actually wore the 'Action Press' uniform states that about 15 members of his branch wore the uniform: he remembers that the left-wing opposition thought they were a highly trained superforce and gave them a wide berth. He considers this style of uniform was one of the factors which encouraged the Government to ban the wearing of political uniforms.[23]

An ex-Blackshirt from Clapham South London, recalls travelling on the underground with local members to the subsequently banned East London March on October 4th 1936. In his group from Clapham Branch, 7 or 8 were wearing the 'Action Press' uniform, it was the first occasion he had worn the Blackshirt uniform and he was the only one wearing a fencing tunic!.[24]

A former Richmond-upon-Thames Surrey, Blackshirt who wore the 'Action Press' uniform himself mentions that all the officers of his branch wore the uniform.[25] Although this is obviously a small sample it does indicate how widely the uniform was worn.

The 'Action Press' uniform was variously described as a 'Police style' uniform and even as an 'Army uniform' by the press. The 'Sunday Referee'[26] correctly pointed out its similarity to the uniforms of the Guards regiments, particularly mentioning the button group arrangement.

---

22   Arthur Wilson. Interview. May 18th 1984.

23   Reg Buck. Correspondence October 1990.

24   John Warburton. Interview October 24th 1998.

25   Charles Hall. Recorded interview. F.O.M. archives.

26   *Sunday Referee*. October 11th 1936.

The Men's 'Action Press' Uniform

The men's 'Action Press' uniform consisted of a black officer's type peaked cap, bearing white embroidered emblems of a Flash and Circle above a Fasces on a black cloth patch. A black undress shirt and tie was worn under a military style jacket of a Melton fabric with four pockets. The jacket had silver metal buttons bearing a flash, these were worn in a similar grouping to the Guards regiments.

A standard B.U.F. red, white and blue, Flash and Circle brassard was stitched to the upper left arm of the jacket. A wide black leather belt was worn with a large nickel-plated buckle on which was mounted a silver Fasces badge. This rested on metal belt hooks on either side of the jacket. A pair of dove grey riding breeches of cotton hair cord finished with a thin black stripe down each outer seam were also worn. Black leather knee boots completed the outfit. An alternative to the riding breeches in the form of grey trousers to be worn with black shoes was available to Inspecting Agents and District Agents.

'Action Press' uniform jacket.

March to Finsbury Park. 1936.

Accrington. 1936.

Sir Oswald Mosley's 'Action Press' uniform differed from the regulation uniform in two ways. On each jacket sleeve cuff were three small silver buttons bearing the lightning flash. Also the embroidered badges on his cap, although keeping to the basic design were of a slightly different appearance and may possibly have been hand embroidered.

Men's Action Press uniform cap.

Embroidered men's cap badge.

Uniform button.

Men's Action Press breeches.

Men's Action Press boots.

Blackshirt being fitted with 'Action Press' uniform. October 1936.

The Women's 'Action Press' Uniform

The women's 'Action Press' uniform consisted of a close-fitting pillbox type hat bearing an embroidered triangular shaped badge on which was a Flash and Circle emblem above a number one. A black fencing tunic was worn with a B.U.F. brassard on the upper left arm. A wide black leather belt was worn the same as the men's and a grey skirt and black shoes completed the uniform.

Women members of the B.U.F. 1936.

Women's cloth hat badge.

Women's 'Action Press' hat, 1936.

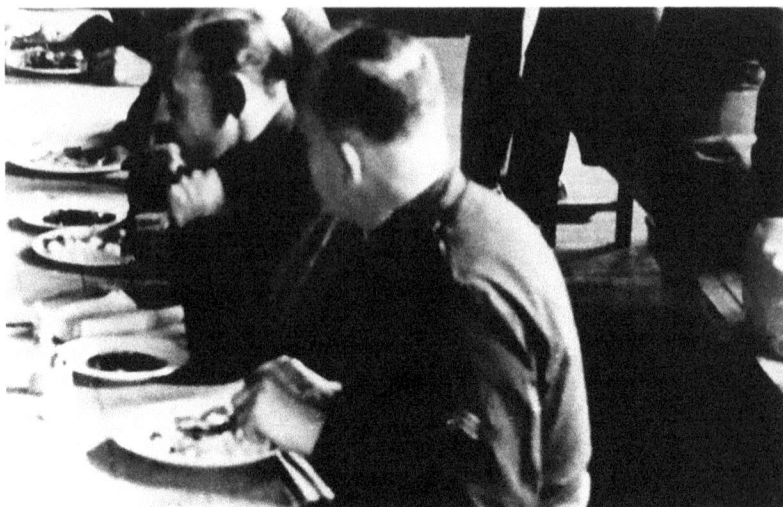

Photograph of a Senior Unit Leaders rank insignia being worn in the Black House canteen in 1933.

Insignia of Defence Force Unit Leader, 1933.

Badges of Rank

Men's Badges of Rank 1933 – 1935

The B.U.F. introduced its unique rank structure with its distinctive flash insignia early in its existence: the earliest information available is in the form of a 'Fascist HQ. Bulletin' of October 1933. There is however no way of knowing how long these regulations had been in force.

Fascist H.Q. Bulletin. October 1933

Badges of Rank

Officers are distinguished by a flash of different colours, worn on the left breast as follows.

Red Flash	Senior Staff Officer
Gold Flash	Staff Officer
Blue Flash	Deputy Staff Officer
White Flash	Administrative Officer
Green Flash	Branch Organiser
Purple Flash	Propaganda Officer
Three Stripes	Senior Unit Leader
Two Stripes	Unit Leader, Defence Force

The six B.U.F. badges of rank.

The above listing failed to mention one rank in use at this time, that of Deputy Administrative Officer (D.A.O.). Following the military practice each rank covered a number of positions.

The flash rank badges were embroidered cotton on a black woollen base and in this early period were worn almost horizontally on the left breast of the black shirt tunic. The Defence Force insignia of Senior Unit Leader and Unit Leader were worn on the upper left arm of the uniform: from photographs they would appear to be embroidered chevrons on a black background. Although not mentioned in the bulletin the colour of the Defence Force insignia was almost certainly gold.

The growth of the B.U.F. in 1933 necessitated by November the introduction of a new much expanded rank structure. No less than 23 new ranks were created of which 21 had their own insignia. A further two ranks were added five months later! It is unlikely that many of the senior ranks of either the Defence Force or Administration were in fact ever used. For example, Eric Hamilton Peircy, the senior Defence Force officer, only ever attained the rank of 3rd Commander and never appears to have worn any rank insignia. The Chief of Staff Ian Hope Dundas wore his badge of rank of crossed Fasces surmounted by a lion's head in gilt wire on the left breast of his tunic. The same insignia also featured on a scarlet brassard worn on his upper left arm. The scarlet brassard was at some period replaced by a black brassard, and this continued to be worn until 1935.

The White markings given for Administration would seem to have been short lived. Once again due to the lack of documentation I have had to rely on the memories of former B.U.F. members which obviously after so many years can be faulty. The propaganda markings at some stage ceased to be regarded as ranks and became simply indications of the proficiency of the speaker. As the speaker became more proficient he or she was entitled to address further types of meetings, and was awarded a further Purple bar. It has been stated by a former B.U.F. speaker that by late 1934 the Propaganda bars and flashes were being worn on the upper sleeve of the left arm of the black shirt tunic.[27] Originally the insignia like that of Defence and Administration was worn on the left breast. There is some evidence that badges for Sales Officers were worn for a very short time in November 1934, these took the form of a green flash, and one, two, and three green bars. However, there are no details as to what specific ranks these represented.

---

27   Reg Buck. Correspondence. October 1990.

B.U.F. OFFICIAL GAZETTE.[28]

The following are the new markings for all Officers of the British Union of Fascists. As from 17th November 1933 at 6am, ALL present ranks of the British Union of Fascists are hereby cancelled.

DEFENCE		ADMINISTRATION	
1 Gold Bar	Unit Leader	Sub-Branch Officer	1 White Bar
2 Gold Bars	Section Leader	Deputy Branch Officer	2 White Bars
3 Gold Bars	Sub-Company Officer	Branch Officer	3 White Bars
Gold Flash	Company Officer	Deputy-Administrative Officer	White Flash
Gold Flash & 1 Gold Bar	Sub-Commandant	Administrative Officer	White Flash & 1 White Bar
Gold Flash & 2 Gold Bars	Commandant	Area Administrative Officer	White Flash & 2 White Bars
Gold Flash & 3 Gold Bars	Sub-Commander	Senior Administrative Officer	White Flash & 3 White Bars
Red Flash	3rd Commander	No equivalent in Administrative Section	
Red Flash & 1 Gold Bar	2nd Commander	Zone Administrative Officer	Blue Flash & 1 White Bar
Red Flash & 2 Gold Bars	1st Commander	National Administrative Officer	Blue Flash & 2 White Bars

---

28   *Fascist News.* November 17th 1933.

PROPAGANDA

1 Purple Bar	Assistant Propaganda Officer
Purple Flash	Propaganda Officer
Purple Flash & 1 Purple Bar	Senior Propaganda Officer
Purple Flash & 2 Purple Bars	National Propaganda Officer

Ian Dundas. Chief of Staff will wear a lion and crossed Fasces.

Dr Robert Forgan. Deputy C-in-C (Defence Force) will wear no badge

Sir Oswald Mosley. Commander in Chief (Defence Force) will wear no badge.

A 'Headquarters Bulletin' was issued in late November 1933 outlining how the new rank structure would affect individual branches.

B.U.F. HEADQUARTERS BULLETIN.[1]
DEFENCE FORCE

Section Leader to wear 2 Gold Bars. Unit Leader to wear 1 Gold Bar.

Where a Branch Defence Force is too small to form One Section (ie.27 men, 3 Unit Leaders, 1 Section Leader), the rank should be :

DEFENCE FORCE		ADMINISTRATION
(Gold)		(White)
Unit Leader	1 Bar	Sub-Branch Officer

As soon as the Branch reaches the position of establishing One Section, then recommendation should be forwarded to N.H.Q. for promotions to fill the vacancies of: -

DEFENCE FORCE		ADMINISTRATION
(Gold)		(White)
Section Leader	2 Bars	Deputy Branch Officer
Unit Leader (3)	1 Bar	Sub-Branch Officer

---

1   *Fascist News.* November 25th 1933.

Where a Branch has a Defence Force of sufficient strength to allow of forming of Two Sections, (a Section consisting of 27 men, 3 Unit Leaders, 1 Section Leader, in all 31 active): then the appointment of a Sub- Company Officer (3 Gold Bars) should be recommended to N.H.Q., and the Officer-in-Charge of the Branch, now wearing 2 White Bars, should be recommended for promotion to Branch Officer wearing 3 White Bars.

DEFENCE FORCE		ADMINISTRATION
(Gold)		(White)
Sub-Company Officer	3 Bars	Branch Officer
Section Leader	2 Bars	Deputy Branch Officer
Unit Leader	1 Bar	Sub-Branch Officer

PROPAGANDA DEPARTMENT

Propaganda Officer to wear a Purple Flash.

Assistant Propaganda Officer to wear 1 Purple Bar.

The Officer-in-Charge of Branch Propaganda to be an Assistant Propaganda Officer, and wear 1 Purple Bar.

March 1934

A further two Propaganda ranks were added in March 1934.

PROPAGANDA RANKS

Two new ranks will come into force on March 1st 1934. These will be: -

3 Purple Bars	Deputy Propaganda Officer
2 Purple Bars	Assistant Deputy Propaganda officer.

By order, Ian.H.Dundas. Chief of Staff.[2]

---

2   *The Blackshirt*. February 16th-22nd 1934.

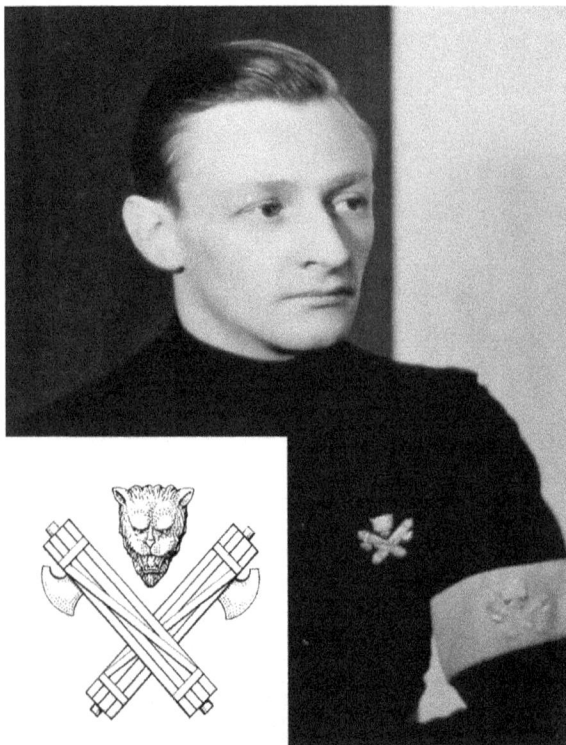

Ian Hope Dundas the B.U.F. Chief-of-Staff wearing this insignia c. 1935.

BUF Chief-of Staff wearing the black brassard which replaced the earlier scarlet brassard.

Men's Badges of Rank 1935 – 1936

Although the rank descriptions changed during the reorganisation of the Movement in early 1935, the insignia remained basically the same. The rank details published in the British Union Constitution and Regulations of May 1936, (see illustration) had been in force since May 1935, although several changes to the design of insignia occurred in 1936. For instance the original type of rank flash was replaced with a reversed version, the reason for this is unknown.

Neil Francis-Hawkins was appointed Director of Blackshirt Organisation in early 1935, but it was not until the autumn that a badge of rank for this position was adopted. When he became Director-General of Organisation in January 1936, he continued to wear this insignia. The unique badge featured a Fasces and lightening flash, which crossed diagonally, in a wreath of oak leaves, surmounted by a lions head. He later wore a smaller version of this insignia on the shoulder straps of his 'Action Press' uniform; these black straps were bordered in red.

Director-General of Organisation Rank Insignia

Area Administrative Officer Lt. Col. Crocker, 1934.

District Inspector E.G. 'Mick' Clarke, 1936.

Badges of Rank

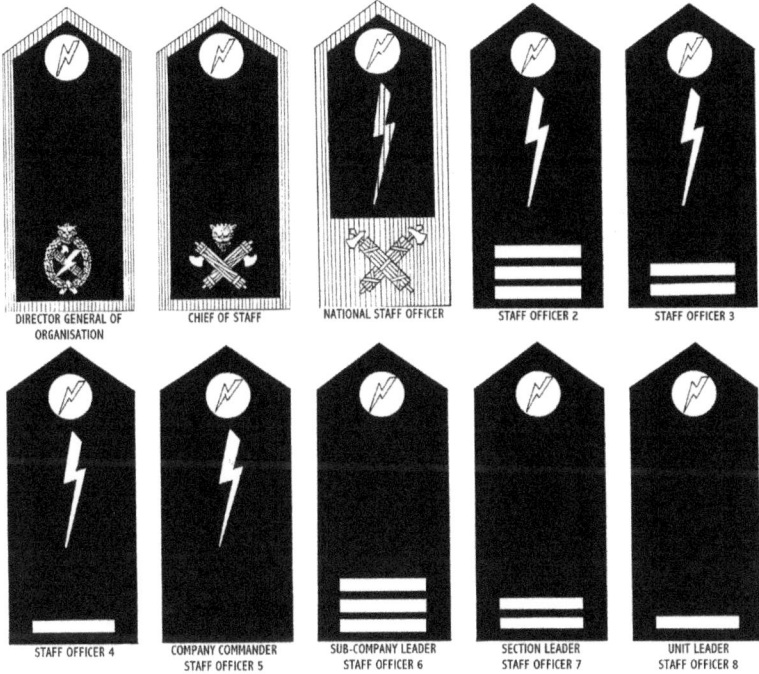

| DIRECTOR GENERAL OF ORGANISATION | CHIEF OF STAFF | NATIONAL STAFF OFFICER | STAFF OFFICER 2 | STAFF OFFICER 3 |

| STAFF OFFICER 4 | COMPANY COMMANDER STAFF OFFICER 5 | SUB-COMPANY LEADER STAFF OFFICER 6 | SECTION LEADER STAFF OFFICER 7 | UNIT LEADER STAFF OFFICER 8 |

The B.U.F rank insignia as worn on the shoulder straps
of the 'Action Press' uniform during 1936

Alexander Raven Thomson wearing the 'Action Press' uniform - 1936. His rank insignia can be seen on the shoulder straps of his uniform. At this time he was the B.U.F.'s Director of Publicity.

Section IV - Officers

1. Classification of Officers

(77)   Officers will be classified as follows:-

RANK	APPOINTMENT	BADGE	
National Staff Officer	Chief Executive and Administrative Officers	⚡	(Red)
Staff Officer 2	National Inspecting Officers and senior executive appointments	⚡ ≡	(Gold)
Staff Officer 3	Assistant National Inspecting Officers	⚡ ＝	(Gold)
Staff Officer 4	N.H.Q. Organising Officers District Inspecting Officers County Propaganda Officers	⚡ —	(Gold)
Company Commander Staff Officer 5	District Officers District Treasurers Company Commanders	⚡	(Gold)
Sub-Company Leader Staff Officer 6	Deputy District Officers	≡	(Gold)
Section Leader Staff Officer 7	Acting District Officers Section Leaders	＝	(Gold)
Unit Leader Staff Officer 8	Acting District Officers Unit Leaders	—	(Gold)

(78)   **Ranks and Appointments**

Every officer in the Movement will hold substantive rank. When holding an appointment, an officer will be given the temporary rank of the appointment and when vacating it will revert to substantive rank.

'Badges of Rank' from the Constitution and Regulations published May 1936.

Clement Bruning, Administrative Officer Southern Propaganda wears the most senior Speakers grade badge. October 1936.

1.—Plan your speech in outline and be certain of your facts.

2.—Speak slowly and distinctly. The most brilliant speech is useless if it is not understood.

3.—Always remember the purpose of your speech, which is to gain sympathy and support for the movement, not to entertain the already converted.

4.—Always answer questions courteously. All questioners are not hostile.

5.—Never lose your temper—it is fatal.

6.—Don't spend too much time condemning your opponents. Be constructive.

7.—Don't be clever at the expense of your audience. They have the last word at the polls.

8.—Don't talk too much about foreign countries. That is their business. Ours is " Britain First."

THE BRITISH UNION.

SPEAKER'S WARRANT.

Mr. Robert Saunders
Friar Mayne Farm
Broadmayne Dorchest.

This is to certify that the holder of this warrant has been registered as a Speaker competent to represent the British Union in accordance with the conditions specified below :

Authorisation

1.—National Indoor Meetings.

2.—National Outdoor Meetings.

3.—Small Indoor Meetings.   X   CB

4.—Factory Gate Meetings.   X

5.—Learned Societies and Business Men's Luncheons.

6.—Women's Afternoon Mt'gs.   X

7.—Private Invitation Meetings.   X   CB

8.—Ordinary Outdoor Meetings.   X

GRADING.

Date : 1-4-36
Grade : VI

Date : 1-1-37
Grade : V

Date : 14-10-37
Grade : IV   CB

Date : 8 3 3y.
Grade : III

Date :
Grade :

Date :
Grade :

Signed Clement Bruning
Propaganda Administrator.

A Speakers Warrant card of the type issued from 1936 onwards.

Speakers Badges 1936

The B.U.F proposed to introduce badges for the Movements graded speakers in 1936, however, because of the Public Order Act coming into force in January 1937 this never took place. There is evidence that Clement Bruning, Administrative Officer Southern Propaganda, actually wore a speakers badge, this was the version with crossed torches and a scroll which he wore on his upper left arm on October 4th 1936, when he was photographed in Royal Mint Street before the proposed East London march. However, no evidence has come the light of any other speaker wearing a similar badge of any sort.

The British Union Constitution and Regulations as early as May 1936 stated that badges would be awarded to speakers along with their warrant card although this did not take place. Six different badges are known to exist and are shown below.

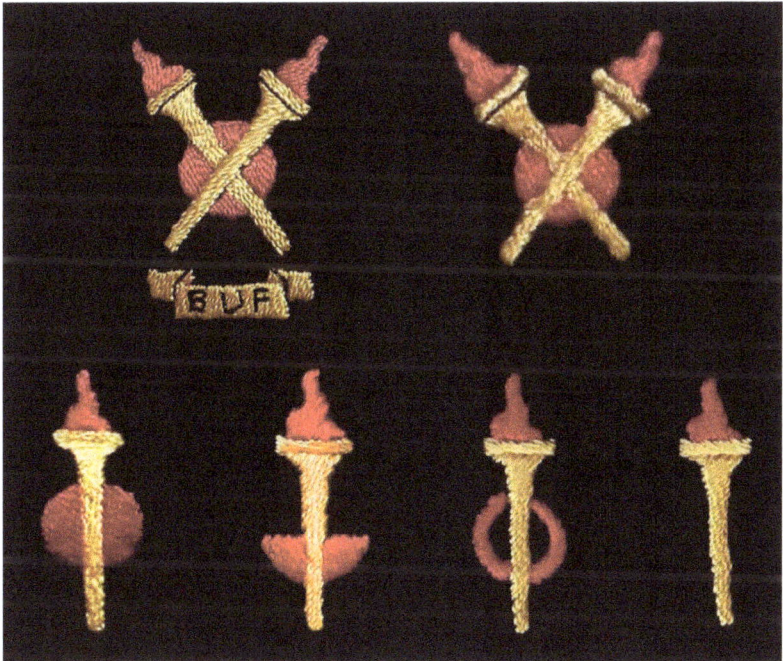

Speakers badges. Most senior grades top row from left, then bottom row from left.

Mosley's Men in Black

One Gold Bar (in use 1933-1935)
Assistant Women's Organiser (Equivalent to Men's Unit Leader)

Two Gold Bars (in use 1933-1935)
Women's Organiser (Equivalent to Men's Section Leader)

Two Gold Bars and One Gold Star
Area / Regional rank including Women's Area Organiser & Area Inspectors.

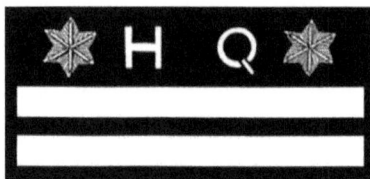

Two Gold Bars and Two Gold Stars
With letters HQ. (Women's Executive Officer based at Women's HQ

Two Gold Bars and Three Stars with letters H.Q. below which are letters C.O.
Director of Organisation of the Women's Section.
(Maud Lady Mosley held this position 1933-1935).

Miss Marjorie Aitken was appointed Commandant of the 'Women's Defence
Force' (also referred to as the Women's Defence Corps) on the 19th April 1934.
Above is an artists impression of her unique badge of rank.

Womens Badges of Rank 1933 – 1935

To my knowledge no B.U.F. documentation relating to the various rank structures of the Women's Section has survived. Consequently the following information has been mainly obtained from former members. Period photographs have also been helpful in showing the rank insignia actually being worn. In the early period the women's rank insignia featured bars and stars which were worn above the left breast pocket on the blouse. Women members of the Special Propaganda Section, who like the men wore the Black shirt tunic, wore their rank insignia on the left breast.

Only the one colour Gold (except for women speakers) would appear to have been used, and the women's rank bars were much longer and thicker than those used for the men's insignia. Women Propaganda officers (speakers) during this period wore the same Purple insignia as the men: originally on the breast and later on the upper sleeve of the left arm. The tentative rank structure (left) was in use from 1933 until early 1935.

Women's Executive Officer based at Women's Headquarters. The woman wears a variant of the normal badge.

Maud Lady Mosley wearing her rank insignia.

Women's District officer wearing the stylised letter 'W' rank insignia.

These rank badges appear to be genuine, but the significance of the different colour is not known. They are at variance to the normal colour gold which was used.

Women's Badges of Rank 1935 – 1936

Like the rest of the B.U.F. organisation, the Women's Section underwent far-reaching reforms in early 1935. One aspect of these changes was that some titles and rank insignia were altered. The women adopted shorter and smaller embroidered rank bars; by 1936 these took the form of a stylised letter W. Below is a tentative outline of the Women's Section rank insignia constructed from the information available.

One Gold bar	Assistant Women's District Officer (Women's Team Leader)
Two Gold bars	Women's District Officer (Women's Canvass Officer)
Three Gold bars	Women's Executive Officer (Women's Propaganda Officer) (Senior Women's Canvass Officer)
Three Stylised W's	Women's Administrative Officer above a bar.

Two women held the above rank / position, which was created in 1936 when this type of insignia was introduced. Ann Brock-Griggs was W/A/O (Southern) and Olga Shore W/A/O (Northern) and were the Leaders of the Women's Sections in their respective parts of the country.

Women's Administrative Officer insignia. 1936

Blackshirt Cadet.

Youth Movement

The B.U.F. 'Youth Movement' was originally founded in 1933, and in 1934 a young fascist activist by the name of Loring was appointed National Youth Organiser. The organisation's structure was loose at this stage and only catered for boys. An early attempt to found a girl's section in the summer of 1934 was still born. In this early period some boys are to be seen in photographs wearing the undress Black shirt with a black tie.[29] However, there is no way of knowing if this was official wear. By early 1936 (or possibly late 1935) the Grey shirt had been adopted, but does not at this time seem to have been very widely worn.[30]

On the 20th July 1936 the Mosley 'Youth Movement' was formally re-launched under the title of the 'British Union Youth Movement'. Unlike previous organisations the new B.U.Y.M. was organised nationwide, had a tight organisational structure and came under the control of the British Union Director-General of Organisation.[31] Although girls were involved in this new initiative no details of their involvement appears in official documents, indicating that perhaps the number of female members was very small. The B.U.Y.M. was split into two sections: The Blackshirt Cadets for young men aged 14-18 years and the Fascist Youth for boys aged 9-14 years.

The Blackshirt Cadets

The Blackshirt Cadets were organised into Units, Sections and Companies with the same numerical strength as the adult Movement. Units (and larger formations where they existed) were commanded by a Cadet member, with the word Cadet prefixed to his rank, i.e. Cadet Unit Leader, Cadet Section Leader, etc. All Cadet ranks were only operative within The Blackshirt Cadets and no Cadet officer had any authority over members of the adult Movement. The design of the Blackshirt Cadet rank badges are shown overleaf. Blackshirt Cadet rank insignia featured white bars on a black background.

---

29   See photograph in *The Blackshirt*. November 18th-24th 1933. Page 3.

30   See photograph in *The Blackshirt*. March 28th 1936.

31   *The Blackshirt*. July 18th 1936.

CADET UNIT LEADER

CADET SECTION LEADER

CADET SUB-COMPANY
LEADER

CADET COMPANY
COMMANDER

CADET UNIT LEADER

The official uniform regulations for the Blackshirt Cadets are given as follows:

> Grey shirt with patch pockets and black shoulder straps. Plain black tie, grey flannel trousers, broad Fascist belt, forage cap, black shoes or boots.
>
> The circle and flash (embroidered, gold flash on black ground) to be worn on pleat of pocket on left side of shirt.
>
> Shirtsleeves to be worn rolled up above the elbows, (rolled on the outside).
>
> Rank Badges will be worn on the left breast of the uniform'.[32]

The Forage cap proved to be no more popular with the Cadets than it had with their adult counter parts, and apart from Cadet bandsmen was rarely worn.

The B.U.F. brassard was quite extensively worn by Cadets with their Grey shirt uniform, and like the adult Movement this does not seem to have been compulsory.

---

32   Document titled *Organisation of Youth Movement.*

The Fascist Youth

The Fascist Youth were organised in Teams of not more than a Team Leader and five members, each Team was attached to a Unit of the adult Movement. Fascist Youth rank insignia was white letters on a black background. The design of the Fascist Youth rank badges is given below.

'As for the Cadets, but grey shorts may be worn, grey stockings with black tops, a narrow belt with Fascist buckle to be substituted for the ordinary belt, no cap will be worn'.

TEAM LEADER

GROUP LEADER (SENIOR TEAM LEADER IN DISTRICT)

Fascist Youth on Parade.

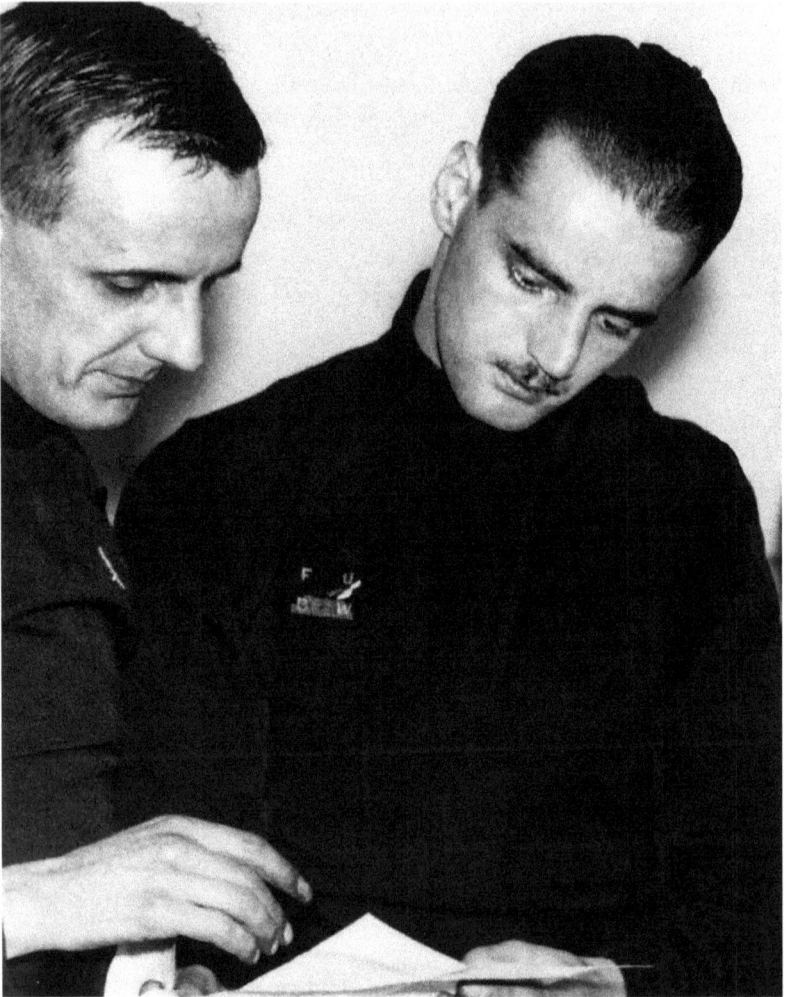

Photograph from 1933 showing the cloth F.U.B.W. patch being worn on the right breast.

Fascist Union of British Workers

The F.U.B.W. was founded in Battersea, South London, in late 1932 as a Fascist organisation for the unemployed and to counter the communist 'National Unemployed Workers Movement'. Originally the F.U.B.W was an independent organisation and membership was possible without joining the B.U.F. However by February 1933 the organisation had been incorporated into the B.U.F. becoming it's industrial arm. *The Blackshirt* newspaper of that month reported Brown shirted F.U.B.W. members as being active on the streets of Battersea.[33] A former B.U.F. member states, that their Brown shirt uniform was actually more of a khaki colour and was worn with a black tie and grey trousers.[34] By spring 1933 F.U.B.W. members were wearing the normal B.U.F. Black Shirt with the union's cloth badge on the right breast of the tunic.

F.U.B.W. embroidered badge.

F.U.B.W. membership badge for wear in civilian clothes.

In May 1934 a Home Office report on F.U.B.W. activities mentions members at this date wearing their embroidered cloth badge on the upper arm of the tunic. A small enamel membership badge was worn in civilian clothes. The F.U.B.W. was incorporated into the Industrial Section of the B.U.F 's Propaganda Department in the summer of 1934.

---

33   *The Blackshirt*. February 1933.

34   John Warburton. Correspondence 1994.

Mosley speaks to supporters Hyde Park, London.

A 1933 photograph showing the FUBW cloth badge being worn on the shoulder, also on the right a member of the Fascist Police is shown wearing a scarlet brassard bearing Fasces and initials F.P.

Special Brassards

Special brassards were used from the earliest days of the B.U.F. to indicate that the wearer held a supervisory or executive position This was especially the case during the days when the B.U.F. N.H.Q. was based at the huge Black House complex in Chelsea. Originally the brassards were worn on the upper right arm but by late 1933 this had been changed to the upper left arm.

Fascist Police.

"Fascist Police act as do Military Police and have full authority when on duty. They wear a scarlet brassard with the letters 'F.P.' inscribed, and are responsible for seeing that the conduct of members conforms with standing orders, both inside B.U.F. premises and in certain districts." (Fascist HQ. Bulletin. 11th November 1933). Photographs show the brassard being worn on the upper left arm with a gold Fasces badge between the letters F and P.

Executive Officer

"A red armband with gold Fasces with the words 'Executive Officer' to be worn when on duty".(B.U.F. Standing Orders. 20th December 1934.) This refers to the Executive Officer at B.U.F. N.H.Q. (Black House). The brassard almost certainly follows the same design as the London Command brassard; this had a central Fasces and the words above and below. Other red brassards are known to have been used, including Guard commander and Orderly Officer.

March Officials

On major London marches in the late 1930's a Green armband without insignia was worn by the Propaganda Administrator (E.G. 'Mick'Clarke)[35] In the same period March Detachment Leaders wore a numbered yellow brassard.[36]

---

35   Order of March. May 7th 1939.

36   Order of March. May 7th 1939.

First Aid Section

B.U.F. First Aid Units wore various types of brassards with the Black shirt uniform. One type bore a white cross on a red armband, another featured a white cross in a circle . First aiders in 'Action Press' uniform wore a first aid brassard in place of the Movements Flash and Circle brassard.

A 1935 photograph of a Blackshirt wearing a First Aider's brassard, what is of special interest is the fact the brassard has the initials L.F.A.C, this signifies that that he is a member of the 'London Command First Aid Company', presumably this had been shortened to the four letters. It is of interest that this company also had their own standard, the brass top had the letters L.C.F.A.C., with the banner being awarded in March 1935.

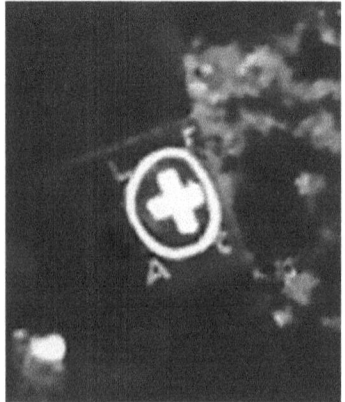

London Command

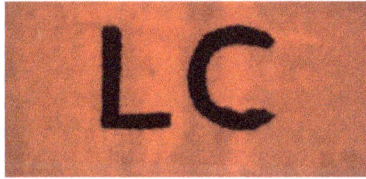

A brassard for the Officer in charge of 'London Command' followed the same general pattern as those above. This was a red brassard with a central gold wire Fasces with the words 'London' above and 'Command' below also in gold wire. There was another version of this brassard; this had the letters 'L.C.' in black chain stitch on a red armband. With the change from military terminology on the passing of the 1936 Public Order Act, the 'London Command' was re-titled 'London Administration'. On B.U.F. marches in the late 1930's, Capt. U.A. Hick, Senior Administrator London Administration, wore a brassard as above only bearing the words 'London Administration'.

Transport Section

The Transport Section based at Black House was responsible for the rapid transport of speakers and defence units in London. When on duty members wore a plain blue armband with their Black shirt. Officer's brassards featured a badge that appears to be a side view of a wheel, with a wing protruding from each side. A similar badge was worn on the peaked cap of some drivers. In June 1934 the London Volunteer Transport Section was formed, this organisation supplemented the Transport Section and assisted in the transport of speakers and defence units. It was later extended to include the provision of cars for staff officers and the Medical Section: members provided their own cars and paid their own costs. A report of a B.U.F. parade in March 1935 describes the presence of L.V.T.S. members wearing blue armbands.

Ticket to the Earls Court 'Britain First' rally, July 1939.

Van in East London selling tickets to the Earls Court rally, June 1939.

Earls Court Rally

Senior officials at the B.U.F. Earls Court Rally on 16th July 1939 wore special brassards. The hall was divided into sections; the official in charge of each section wore a brassard of the same colour as the button badge worn by stewards in that part of the hall. The colours were Red, White, Blue, Brown, Green and Yellow. Senior officials in control of the meeting wore a standard type B.U.F. Flash and Circle brassard but with an added white stripe going through the centre.

The Mass Colours entering Trafalgar Square after a march from Kentish Town, July 4th 1937. Note flag carried on right.

Flags, Standards and Banners

During its existence the B.U.F. used flags, standards, and banners of various designs. A unique Fascist flag was used from the official launch of the B.U.F. At the inaugural ceremony on the 3rd October 1932 at the former New Party offices in Great George Street, Westminster, Sir Oswald Mosley unfurled this flag from the roof of the building. The colours of this flag are unknown for certain. This flag made a further appearance at the first B.U.F. Rally in Trafalgar Square on the 15th October 1932. After this date it does not seem to have been used again.

Sir Oswald Mosley raises the Fascist flag in Great George Street, October 1932.

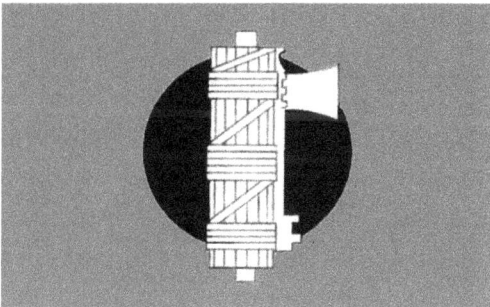

The original Fasces flag 1932.

Women's H. Q. c1933. Shown on the wall is a variant of the official black and gold flag introduced in 1933.

Fascist supporters salute Oswald Mosley. July 4th 1937.

The Fascist Flag 1933 – 1940

In early 1933 the B.U.F. introduced a new Fasces flag that they were to use until the disbanding of the Movement in 1940. This flag was in the new official colours of gold and black, and consisted of a gold lightening flash passing through a central gold Fasces on a black field. This large flag was made of black cotton material, with the Fasces and lightening flash being laid on gold coloured canvass. The Movement used this flag extensively and each local branch possessed a flag of this type which was carried alongside the Union flag at both local and national events. It was on this flag that the distinctive brass pole tops of the B.U.F's London Districts and special formations were carried. Each London branch (from 1935 known as a district) carried a Fascist flag pole topped by a cut out brass plaque bearing the name of the branch. This was surmounted by a brass letter L, the code letter for London, inside a circle.

A number of provincial districts in the late 1930's are shown in photographs to be using pole tops of the same type as the London Districts, only using the code letters S for the Southern area and N for the Northern area inside a circle. This however does not seem to have been very widespread. Other B.U.F. Sections used similar type pole tops, including the Women's, Cadet's, and First Aid sections to name a few. The main difference to the London tops is that the Flash and Circle was used in place of the London code letter. *Action*[37] reported that the following banners representing various B.U.F. Industrial Sections were carried at the Earls Court Rally of July 1939: Transport workers, Clerical workers, Mine workers, Land workers and Metal workers. Banner tops are also known to have existed for the Cab Trade and the Catering trade.

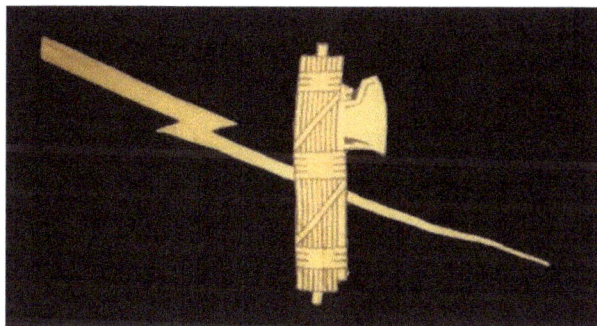

Fascist flag 1933 – 1940

---

37   *Action*. July 22nd 1939.

London District flag pole top.

Women's Section flag pole top.

The BUF Colours at London Bridge during the 1938 May Day march.
Note London District flag pole tops.

The bottom section of a London District flag pole top.

The Rome Presentation Standard

During the visit to the International Fascist Exhibition in Rome, in April 1933 Achille Starace, Secretary of the Fascist Grand Council of the Italian Fascist Party (P.N.F.), presented the B.U.F. delegation led by Sir Oswald Mosley with a gift of a unique standard.

The standard finial depicted a spread eagle in the centre of a wreath above a rectangular tablet. Suspended from a horizontal cross-bar by five loops hung an oblong black standard cloth, this had a central embroidered silver Fasces emblem and the wording "British Union of Fascists" and "For King - Empire and International Justice". At the top left hand corner of the cloth was a small Union Jack and the standard was finished with silver tassels and fringe.

The BUF delegation posing with the Rome Presentation Standard. The standard bearer Eric Hamilton Piercy is flanked by Oswald Mosley and Achille Starace.

The Rome Presentation Standard.

The Leader's Banner

Beginning in 1937, at major London marches and rallies attended by Sir Oswald Mosley, he would be accompanied by his Leader's banner (sometimes described as the Leader's flag). George Armsden, an East London District Leader, always carried this banner.

George Armsden carries the Leader's banner, 1937.

The description 'Leader's banner' applies to three banners used in the years 1937 to 1939. Each was unique, although the two earlier banners followed a similar design. The banner used in 1939 however was radically different in that the cloth section had a fish tail shape.

The first Leader's banner was soon superseded by a second design in late 1937, this in turn was used throughout 1938. This banner was slightly changed during that year, the large flash and circle in a circle of oak leaves on the banner top being replaced with a reversed flash. At the British Union May Day March of the 7th May 1939, Armsden performed his usual function but on this occasion carried one of the new Honour Standards.

A new version of the Leader's banner was introduced in 1939 and seems to have been carried only once at the Earls Court rally in July 1939. After being paraded down the centre aisle by George Armsden the banner was placed at the base of the speaker's plinth. To my knowledge none of these banners survive.

George Armsden holds the Leaders banner which was used in 1938, the 'Flash and Circle' emblem shown was reversed during that year.

LEADER'S BANNER 1937

Leader's Banner 1938
The top section of the banner pole is believed to have been in black and gold, with
the flash and circle finial in silver.

Leader's Banner 1939
Tentative drawing of the Leaders Banner carried at the
Earls Court rally on the 16th July 1939.

British Union Honour Standard

The Honour Standards

The first occasion on which the Honour Standards were to have been carried, was on the Westminster to Shepherds Bush march in October 1938. This event was banned and they were finally paraded in early 1939. The standards were stated by *Action* to have been 'presented to the Movement', and were of a similar design to the two earlier unique Leaders banners, carried in the years 1937 and 1938.

The 60 new standards made their first appearance on the May Day March, from Westminster to Ridley Road, Dalston, on Sunday 7th May 1939. On the march each detachment was headed by four standards. This was the only occasion on which all the standards were carried together on a march, although the full 60 were on display at the huge Earls Court rally on the 16th July 1939 when they were paraded before the 30,000 strong audience. Honour standards were also to be seen at major Peace rallies in the late 1939 and early 1940 period. From July 1939 a number of standards were presented to districts that had shown special merit, this included Islington.[38] Leeds North East, Bournemouth and Derby, the latter displaying their standard at the district bookshop.[39] There were certainly other districts, which received Honour Standards; unfortunately the B.U.F. press contain no information about them.

When the B.U.F. was dissolved in July 1940, a number of Honour Standards were in the possession of local districts, many of these were either lost or seized by the police and destroyed. The majority of the standards were kept in a railway arch store in Haggerstone, East London. During the war this was plundered and items stolen including it is believed some standards. With the foundation of Mosley's post-war 'Union Movement' in 1948, the remaining standards were once again used for marches and rallies with the British Union box section removed.

A former member of staff at the U.M. N.H.Q. states that by 1954 the Movement had less than a dozen Honour Standards in its possession [40] and that the surviving standards disappeared in 1968 when the

---

38   *Action*. July 22nd 1939.

39   *Action*. August 19th 1939.

40   Robert Row. Correspondence February / March 1997.

Ticket to the presentation of an Honour Standard,
13th September 1939. Due to the declaration of war it is
unlikely this event took place.

Honour Standards being carried on the 1939 May Day
March by the 8th London Area.

lease of the U.M. offices in Vauxhall Bridge Road, Victoria, London, expired, necessitating a move to new premises. The standards were temporarily placed in the care of an elderly lady supporter but following her sudden death they were either destroyed or sold surreptitiously by persons unknown.

The Honour Standard consisted of an aluminium pole top of a flash and circle within a circular oak leaf wreath; this was surmounted by a spearhead, this carried an embossed number on its base. Beneath was an oblong box with the raised words BRITISH UNION on both sides. From horizontal black wooden cross bars hung by eight loops, it bore a heavy red ribbed artificial silk-type standard cloth, bearing a flash and circle, the circle being white embroidered oak leaves, the central back-ground is blue again of an artificial silk. The emblem features on one side of the cloth only. The cloth was edged with alternate blue and white wool tassels. The standard staff was a two piece black polished wooden pole.

Red, white and blue Flash and Circle flags being paraded at the B.U.F's Earls Court Rally, July 1939.

A Blackshirt bugler using a large black and gold pennant as a bugle banner. It may be a variant on the normal large car pennant. c.1934.

Other Flags and Banners

From the introduction of the Flash and Circle emblem in 1935, various types of flags bearing this design in red, white and blue were used by the B.U.F. The most commonly used was the 6ft x 3ft size flag as carried at the Earls Court rally of July 1939. These flags were later advertised for sale in *Action* complete with ash pole.[41] Variations on this standard Flash and Circle flag (of which there were many) include a fishtail type, seen in the vanguard of the Movements south London march of May 1938.

A small number of Flash and Circle bugle pennants (see photo below) were produced, and used on marches in the 1939 period, these again were in red, white and blue.

One of the most important flags to be borne at B.U.F. marches and rallies was the 'old flag'. This was a Union Jack in use from the earliest day's of the Movement, and was treated with the utmost reverence District Inspector Walker invariably carried this flag.

Buglers on the B.U.F. North London Regional March, March 12th 1939.

---

41   *Action.* September 2nd 1939.

W.O. Lewis made badge.

1936 type badge with letter F removed.

Prototype B.U.F. lapel badge.

Italian made lapel badge.

The new Blackshirt badge comprising the original fasces super-imposed on a Union Jack. The badge emphasises the patriotism of the movement and will be great assistance to members traveling abroad as indicative of membership of the British Union of Fascists.

- The Fascist Week, March 9th, 1934.

Lapel Badges

During its eight-year existence the B.U.F. produced a variety of lapel badges for wear by members and supporters. Of these only two, the original brass Fasces badge and the Union Jack shield with mounted Fasces could be described as membership badges i.e. badges restricted to B.U.F. members only. Many other badges of various designs were marketed for supporters and sold through such B.U.F. companies as Abbey Supplies Ltd and B.U.F. Trust Stores Ltd. Some districts had made unofficial badges to their own design and these were sold through *Action*. The main manufacturer of B.U.F. metal badges was Roden of Hatton Garden, London, a firm with close B.U.F. connections, and the Birmingham badge makers W.O.Lewis. Small quantities of 'official' badges would also seem to have been manufactured by other firms to meet local district's requirements.

Original gold Fasces lapel badge.

The Gold Fasces was the original badge of the B.U.F., a small brass Fasces lapel badge with a needle pin fixture was introduced on the formation of the Movement in 1932 for wear by members in civilian cloths. Although this badge was replaced in early 1934, it continued to be worn by some members for several years after. The only known maker of this badge was the London firm of Roden, however most badges are unmarked and were made by an unknown manufacturer. A badge of a new design was produced, possibly in late 1933, to replace the original gilt Fasces lapel badge. Although a small number were manufactured it was not adopted by the B.U.F.

In March 1934 [42] a new badge replaced the gold Fasces, it was described by the B.U.F. as having an 'unmistakably British appearance'. It featured a gilded Fasces centrally mounted on a shield shaped enamelled Union Flag, which bore the initials 'B.U.F.' Badges produced after mid 1936 had the letter 'F' removed to reflect the Movement's new title, the 'British Union of Fascists and National Socialists', abbreviated to 'British Union'. The most common makers

---

42   *The Blackshirt* March 9th-15th 1934.

of this badge were Roden and W.O.Lewis. Some badges similar to the above, only with an inverted shield and Italian style Fasces, also exist. They bear an Italian maker's name C.Paccagnini. From photographic evidence it would appear that some B.U.F. members wore badges similar to this design in 1934. The reason for the difference in design is unknown; they could possibly have been manufactured for wear by the many B.U.F. members resident in Italy.

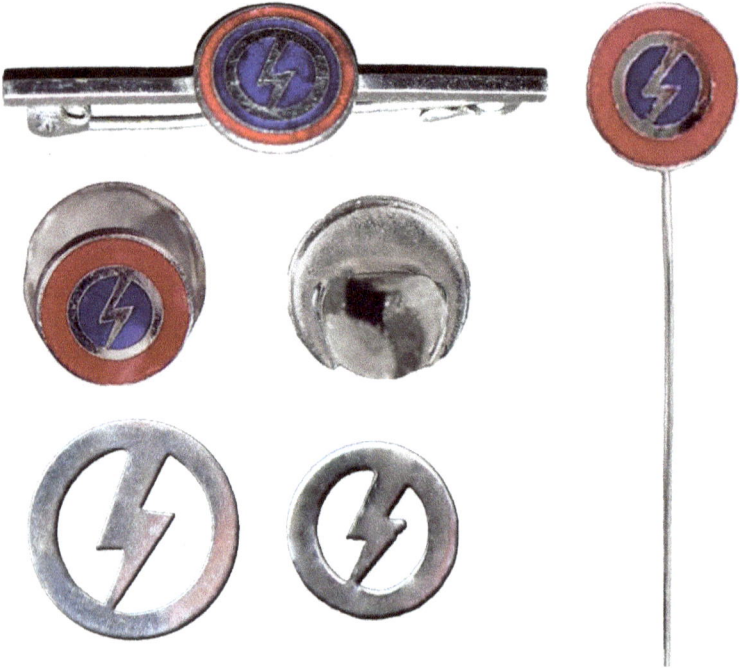

The first metal Flash and Circle badges produced for wear in civilian cloths were made by Tom Nobbs, a B.U.F. jeweller [43] On his own initiative he marketed through *The Blackshirt* from late 1935 a selection of pins and brooches for ladies, including a 1" diameter plain chromium cut out Flash and Circle badge with a button hole fitting. Later 'official' chromium cut out badges of a slightly different design than the earlier brooches were advertised, they came in ½" and ¾" size diameters. A small tie pin was also sold in either chromium or cheaper white metal. These were followed in time by similar badges of various types, including the popular ½" diameter three colour enamelled Flash and Circle badge which was also produced as a brooch for ladies.

43   Tom Nobbs. Interview 1972.

Lapel Badges

In early 1937 a new lapel badge was introduced, described as being "just the thing to be worn during the East End Election campaign" (L.C.C. Election 1937), and in fact was sometimes advertised as an Election favour. This consisted of a red cloth pennant lapel badge, bearing an embroidered Flash and Circle in blue and white. Several versions were available, one with a canvas pennant and cotton embroidered Flash and Circle, another was made of silk and a third type was made from cardboard.

CIRCLE and FLASH LAPEL BADGES

2¼ in. long and 1 in. wide these badges are just the thing to wear during the East End Election Campaign.

3ᴰ·

ABBEY SUPPLIES LIMITED, Sanctuary Buildings, Great Smith Street, Westminster.

'Action' No.52 Feb 13th 1937

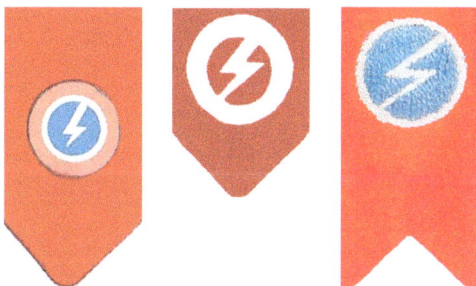

'Mick' Clarke wearing an Election Favour lapel badge during the East London LCC election campaign. 1937.

In 1938 a new buttonhole badge was produced based on a recently designed plaster cast wall plaque of Mosley. The oblong badge featured Mosley's head in profile with the wording 'Our Leader'. Like the plaque it also bore Mosley's signature at the base. The badge was available either with a bronze or silver finish.

BRONZE REPLICAS
OF THE RECENTLY DESIGNED PLAQUE OF
THE LEADER

PRODUCED AS A BUTTONHOLE BADGE
Size 1in. x ⅞in.

PERFECT REPRODUCTIONS **1/-** EACH (Silver Finish 1/6)

NOW ON SALE *Greater Britain Publications*

Action December 3rd 1938

Other lapel badges introduced in the late 1930's included an unofficial Souvenir badge, commemorating the fifth anniversary of the foundation of the B.U.F. in October 1932. A number of cheap 1d and 2d lapel badges were on sale in 1937 including a reproduction of the head of Mosley in cardboard, and a celluloid button badge of the 'Leader portrait'.

Popular fundraisers were small card flags bearing the B.U.F. flag, printed with the event and date i.e. Earls Court 16th July 1939 and May Day 1940.

A particularly popular lapel badge which was sold in large numbers when it was brought out in 1938 was the Supporters badge below. Described as "a replica of the British Union banner finished in red, white and blue".

Finally as previously mentioned some local branches did have their own badges made. One example is Bromley which sold a 'Mind Britain's Business' button badge for the Movement's 'Mind Britain's Business' campaign. This badge was advertised in *Action* in September 1938.

Poster advertising the Earls Court meeting, 16th July, 1939.

Oswald Mosley speaks to an estimated 30,000 supporters at Earls Court, 1939.

Earls Court Rally

Approximately 3,000 B.U.F. members acted as stewards at the huge Earls Court Rally held on the 16th July 1939. This rally, where Mosley spoke to an estimated 30,000 people, was at the time said to have been the largest indoor political meeting ever held in the world.

The stewards wore special tin button badges in six colours - Red, White, Blue, Brown, Green and Yellow. Each colour was worn by 500 stewards and represented a certain section of the hall in which the detachment of stewards wearing that colour was stationed.[44] .

---

44   Stewarding Instructions. B.D.E. Donovan. A.D.G. (A).

Earls Court Rally steward's ticket.

Distinctions

The creation in June 1937 by the B.U.F. of four grades of Distinction for service to the Movement was in response to the passing of the 1936 Public Order Act. This legislation had deprived the B.U.F. of the right to wear uniforms. As special uniforms had been used to reward members who showed sustained commitment to the Movement in political work, so the new Distinctions with their special lapel badges allowed the wearer to be recognised throughout the Movement as one who has "deserved well of the cause". [45]

Uniquely for the B.U.F. very detailed information regarding the Distinctions, including line drawings of the different badges, were printed in *The Blackshirt*.[46] However, it should be noted that several changes were made to the details as originally announced, for instance some of the inscriptions on the badges were either not used or soon altered.

The Distinctions were awarded in four grades ranging from white metal to the gold; each was awarded with a Certificate recording the Leader's appreciation of the recipient's service and devotion to the cause.

The steel badge of the First Division.

The white metal, bronze and gold badge.

The original line drawings of the Distinction badges.
The Blackshirt, June 19th 1937

---

45   *The Blackshirt*. June 19th 1937.

46   *The Blackshirt*, October 2nd 1937.

The Blackshirt June 19th 1937

THE WHITE METAL DISTINCTION

This will be awarded on the recommendation of the District Leader or the District Inspector, to officials and members who have been members for not less than one year and who, in addition have fulfilled one of the following:

(a) Carried out the work of D/L or D/T or any official post in the Organisation of Movement to the satisfaction of the D/I or the N/I for not less than six months.

(b) Sold a minimum of ten papers per week for six months.

(c) Qualified by passing the Agents' Examination, 2nd Class

(d) Enrolled or been responsible for the enrolment of six new members in the six months preceding the recommendation, or of ten members in the year preceding the recommendation.

(e) Given one night per week to systematic canvass for a period of six months

(f) Given regular and reliable service as a speaker during the six months preceding the recommendation.

(g) Collected by means of Contribution Cards a minimum of £5 towards the Election Fund of the District

THE STEEL DISTINCTION

This will be awarded on the recommendation of the D/L or D/I only to officials and members registered as 1st Division Members who have for six months fulfilled the conditions of such membership, and who have in addition sold a minimum of ten papers per week for the same period.

THE BRONZE DISTINCTION

This will be awarded on the recommendation of the D/I who will be entitled to recommend awards on a basis proportionate to the membership and activity of his Inspectorate. The award is for outstanding service to the National Socialist Cause and the following general condition governs it:-

The member recommended must have a minimum of two years service during which time he must have regularly and systematically performed a work of service in a manner which is an example to his District.

THE GOLD DISTINCTION

This will be restricted to ten awards per year. It will be awarded on the recommendation of the Director General for the particularly valuable services over a period of three years OR for the performance of work of exceptional merit for a lesser period.

GENERAL CONDITIONS

The following general conditions and remarks apply to the awards: -

(1) The Distinctions will be retained as long as the member continues to be worthy of it by membership and service.

(2) All members who have been awarded a Distinction of the First or Second grade will be entitled to the letters "D.S" ("Distinguished for Service") after their names in all official documents. All members who have been awarded the Bronze or Gold Distinction will be entitled to the letters "H.S" ("Honoured for Service") after their names in all official documents.

(3) No staff members are to be eligible for any distinction in respect of their paid employment.

(4) The White Metal and Steel Distinctions will be engraved with the initials of the recipient. The Bronze and Gold Distinctions will be engraved with the full name of the recipient and the date of the award.[47]

(5) A certificate of Service and Merit will be issued with each distinction.

(6) Recommendation for the Bronze and Gold Distinction are to be submitted in September each year. All recommendations are to be regarded as confidential and are not to be discussed.

(7) Recommendations for the White Metal and the Steel Distinctions can be submitted at a time when the conditions of the award have been satisfied.

IMPORTANT PRELIMINARY NOTIFICATION

Recommendations for the immediate award of the White Metal and the Steel Distinction can be made at once in respect of members who have since October 1, 1936, fulfilled the conditions of the award. Notification should also be sent to National Headquarters of the names of the members who are at present carrying out one of the conditions of qualification but who have not as yet completed the prescribed period. As other members take up duties, which, if persevered with, will entitle them to the award, their names and the date on which they began that particular service must be sent for registration to H.Q.

---

47   Author's Note: To date I have seen no badge of any grade bearing an engraving.

The Awarding of Distinctions

The first awards of the Distinctions were made in October 1937 on the Fifth Birthday Anniversary of the founding of the B.U.F., although some Certificates have been seen dated late September. On this occasion a list of the names and districts of recipients were printed in *The Blackshirt*.[48] Nine members were listed as receiving the Gold Distinction and thirty-four the Bronze Distinction. It was further stated, "the list is not complete, owing to the late arrival of recommendations from many districts". Lists of the recipients of the lower Steel and White Metal grades were never published, presumably because of the large number involved.

A Supplementary List of Awards was published in January 1938 in *The Blackshirt*.[49] "For conspicuous service on the occasion of the attack on the Leader at Liverpool", four recipients received the Bronze Distinction, including Keller who had taken over speaking at the meeting when Sir Oswald Mosley had been stuck down by a brick.

A second major list of Gold and Bronze Distinction recipients was published in late October 1938 in *Action*.[50] This should have appeared on October 1st, the birthday of the Movement, but had been delayed owing to the Munich crisis. On this occasion one Gold recipient and twenty-four Bronze are listed, a further two names were added to the list of the Bronze Distinction recipients in early November 1938.[51]

By March 1939 Certificates were being numbered in the very low 500's so it is fairly safe to assume that a maximum of approximately 550 Distinctions were awarded during the lifetime of these awards. No further lists appeared in the. B.U.F. newspapers, and with the event of war it is doubtful if any further award of the two higher grades were made. However, the two lower grades continued to be awarded until May 1940.[52]

---

48   *The Blackshirt*. October 2nd 1937.

49   *The Blackshirt*. January 8th 1938.

50   *Action*. October 22nd 1938.

51   *Action*. November 12th 1938.

52   N.H.Q. Instructions by Director-General. Serial No 1164. 6/5/40. ' Service Awards. With the exception of Gold and Bronze, distinctions will be awarded monthly to qualifying members'.

Birthday Honours
For Distinguished Service

BLACKSHIRT

THE PATRIOTIC WORKER'S PAPER

BRITAIN FOR THE BRITISH · No. 231. · October 2, 1937 · Registered at G.P.O. as a newspaper. · Price 1d.

We have very much pleasure in announcing, on this Fifth Birthday Anniversary, the names of members whose magnificent services to the Movement have led to the bestowal upon them of the higher British Union honours. These will be presented to them by the Leader at the forthcoming area conferences.

It should be noted that the list is not complete, owing to the late arrival of recommendations from many districts.

GOLD DISTINCTIONS

W. A. Jenkins, Westminster St. Georges.
Vic-Admiral G. B. Powell, C.M.G., Portsmouth.
W. K. Chambers Hunter, Aberdeen.
W. G. Eaton, Lancaster.
E. H. Adams, Doncaster.
C. F. Watts, London.
Mrs A. Good, Streatham.
Miss L. A. King, London.
Mrs E. Harris, London.

BRONZE DISTINCTIONS

S. Malin, Liverpool Exchange.	E. Dean, London.
W. Howard, Waterloo.	S. Rigby, London
B. F. Lister, Ripon.	Lady S. G. Pearson, Kent.
K. Marsden, Sheffield.	H. P. Rimington, Leeds.
C. Dickenson, Hulme.	W. Denton, Doncaster.
J. A. McDonald, Edinburgh West.	H. Blind, N. E. Essex.
Capt. W. F. Avery, Portsmouth.	C. Finucane, Edinburgh West.
P. Jennings, Oxford.	B. L. Howe, Blackpool.
R. Saunders, Dorset West.	J. S. Beard, Oxford.
W. Sumner, Blackburn.	S. L. Andrews, London.
R, Robert, Withington.	F. Dand, Wolverhampton.
S.T. Dunn, Stoke-on-Trent.	R. Parkyn, Manchester.
Comdr. C.E. Hudson, Chichester.	Miss N. Driver, Burnley.
A Beavan, Upton.	L. Dudley, Elam, Chichester.
Mrs T. A. Ruffcr, London.	A. L. Mason, Limehouse.
Miss F. E. Hayes, Bournemouth.	C. H. Hammond, King's Lynn.
Mrs M. T. Buyliff, Ripon.	R. Jebb, Salisbury.

GOLD

The Gold badge was made of thin 9 ct gold and on the reverse carried a hallmark. The enamel bar was yellow and bore the words FOR MERIT. Originally the enamel bar was to have had the wording FOR SERVICE, however from evidence so far obtained badges with this inscription do not appear to have been produced.

Certificate awarded to Charles Watts District Leader of Westminster (St. Georges).

BRONZE

The Bronze badge was made of a bronze metal, and like the gold distinction had a yellow bar with the wording FOR MERIT. As with the gold badge, it had originally been announced in *The Blackshirt* that the bronze badge would have the wording FOR SERVICE, however no evidence has come to light that badges with this inscription were ever awarded.

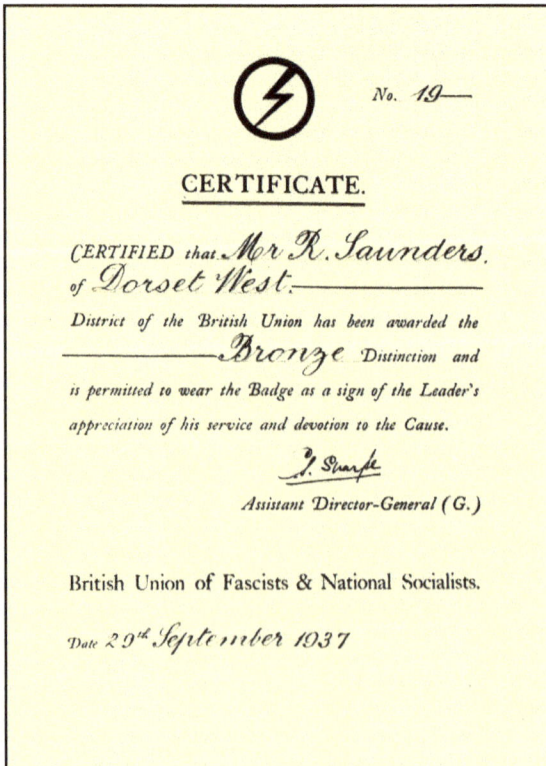

Certificate awarded to Robert Saunders District Leader of Dorset West.

Distinctions

STEEL

The Steel badge with the words TRUE TILL DEATH, bears the original wording. Line drawings were published showing this in June 1937. No reason was given why this later changed to FOR SERVICE. The Steel badge was silver plated bronze; it had a red enamel bar bearing either the wording TRUE TILL DEATH or FOR SERVICE.

No. *363*—

CERTIFICATE.

CERTIFIED that *Mr F. J. Hamley.*
of *Brightside.*————————
District of the British Union has been awarded the
————————————*Steel*—Distinction and
is permitted to wear the Badge as a sign of the Leader's
appreciation of his service and devotion to the Cause.

Assistant Director-General (G.)

British Union of Fascists & National Socialists.

Date *1ˢᵗ October 1938.*

Certificate awarded to Frank Hamley District Leader of Sheffield (Brightside)

117

STEEL (Badge variant)

The Steel badge with FOR SERVICE. Many of these badges bore the makers name 'Roden, 55 Hatton Garden, London E.C.' on the reverse. However, there were certainly other makers.

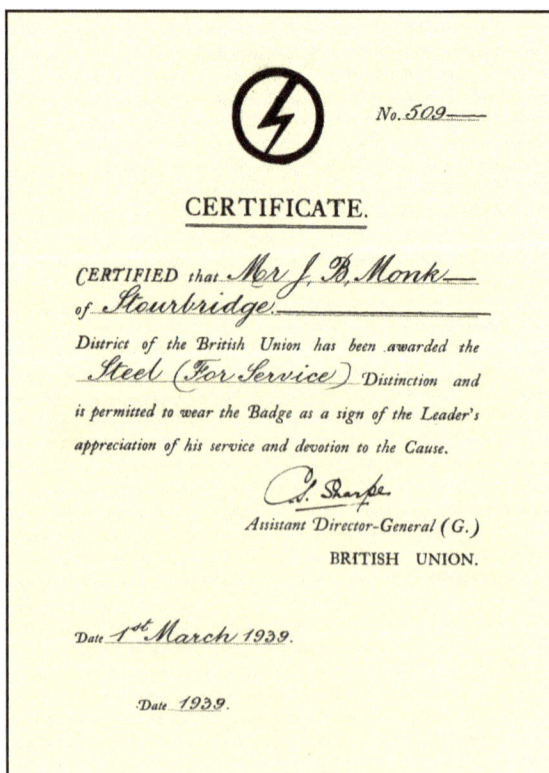

CERTIFICATE.

CERTIFIED that *Mr J. B. Monk* of *Stourbridge.*

District of the British Union has been awarded the *Steel (For Service)* Distinction and is permitted to wear the Badge as a sign of the Leader's appreciation of his service and devotion to the Cause.

Assistant Director-General (G.)

BRITISH UNION.

Date *1st March 1939.*

Date *1939.*

No. *509*

Certificate awarded to J.B. Monk of Stourbridge.

Distinctions

WHITE METAL

.

The White Metal badge like the Steel was silver plated bronze, and had a blue enamel bar with the wording FOR SERVICE.

Certificate awarded to P. Willis Francis one time District Treasurer of Derby.

Women's Drum Corps

Women's Drum Corps

The B.U.F. Women's Drum Corps was formed in late 1938, and first preformed on a march in November of that year. As a band they would seem to have been exempt from the uniform restrictions of the Public Order Act 1936. However it is worth noting that the B.U.F. erred on the side of caution in not putting its male bandsmen into uniform after 1936, an exception to this was the private indoor rally at Earls Court in July 1939. Initially the women wore roll neck navy coloured sweaters often with the Movement's, red, white and blue Flash and Circle brassard on the left arm. Grey or black skirts were worn, usually with the women's narrow uniform belt bearing a small Fasces emblem on the buckle.

At the Earls Court Rally in 1939 the women were fully outfitted in short sleeved navy buttoned shirts with turned down collars, on the right shoulder of which was a small flash badge. A grey skirt was worn with a wide men's uniform belt. This is believed to be the last occasion on which the Women's Drum Corps appeared.

Women's Drum Corps in action, early 1939.

Anne Brock-Griggs, a senior Women's officer wearing a flash tie,
Flash and Circle brooch, and white metal badge. c1938.

B.U.F. Miscellaneous

The B.U.F. and its supporting companies throughout its existence produced a large variety of merchandise. Items bearing the Movement's insignia or Mosley's portrait were popular with the membership and brought in much needed funds. The Greater Britain Publications sales list No 9 (December 1938) illustrated below gives some indication of the wide range of material available. Items on the list were available to the general public, many being sold through the network of Blackshirt bookshops.

It's a

GREATER BRITAIN

Publication

THE FOLLOWING ARE

Greater Britain Publications

Obtainable through any Newsagent or Bookseller or direct from

BRITISH UNION BOOKSHOPS

16, Great Smith Street,	85, Fetter Lane,
WESTMINSTER.	HOLBORN (near Gamages)
Abbey 1704 (6 lines)	Hol. 5689

"**Chosen Race**" **and the British Union** by *Rev. Ellis Roberts, M.A.*
  (3/- per 100, 30/- per 1,000) .. .. ½d.
Education not Conscription by *Oswald Mosley* .. .. .. ½d.
Britain and Jewry .. .. 1d.
Is Lancashire Doomed? .. .. 1d.
Pharmacy, (British Union Policy) .. .. 1d.
A R.P An exposure of the Government's greatest bluff .. 1d.
British Union and the Jews by *E. G. Clarke* (2nd impression)
  Frank statement on British Union's attitude towards the Jew .. 1d.
Motorways for Britain by *A. Raven Thomson*
  A sane and studied contribution to our road problem .. .. 1d.
'**Gainst Trust and Monopoly** by *F. D. Hill* (8th impression)
  British Union Policy for Shopkeepers that has gained widespread support 1d.
Strike Action or Power Action? by *W. Risdon* (2nd impression)
  Shows the disastrous futility of present Trades Union Policy and
  advocates a sound and unanswerable solution .. .. .. 1d.
Taxation and the People by *Oswald Mosley* (2nd impression)
  Popular reprint of two powerful articles on an important subject .. 1d.
Yorkshire Betrayed
  British Union Policy for the Wool Industry .. .. .. 1d.
Lancashire Betrayed
  British Union Policy for the Cotton Industry .. .. 1d.
Slump or Economic Independence? by *A. Raven Thomson*
  A critical analysis of a vital subject .. .. 1d.
Guide to Canvassing (Electoral) .. .. 1d.
Inward Strength of a National Socialist by *Capt. R. Gordon-Canning,*
  M.C. .. .. 1d.
Land and the People by *Jorian Jenks* (3rd impression.)
  Explanation of British Union Agricultural Policy .. .. .. 2d.
Our Financial Masters by *A. Raven Thomson*
  Survey of the Financial System and a statement of British Union Policy 2d.

Lords of the Inland Sea
By *Sir Charles Petre* 10/6
Human Life in Russia
By *Dr. Ammende* (Illustrated) 10/6
Russia in Chains
By *Ivan Solonevich* 12/6
The Windsor Tapestry
By *Compton Mackenzie* .. 16/-
The Spanish Arena 18/-

BOOK REMAINDERS

The Pilgrim of a Smile 1/-
Moscow Mirage 2/-
They Call it Patriotism 3/6
Italian Foreign Policy 5/-
"Conquest of a Continent"
By *Madison Grant* (Pub. 21/-) 6/-
Russian Hazard 6/-
High Speed and Other Flights .. 6/-

SUNDRIES

DECCA RECORDS
Double Sided 1/6
(plus packing and postage 1/-)

Comrades in Struggle } *Oswald Mosley*
British Union

Britain Awake } B.U. Male
The Marching Song } Voice Choir and
Orchestra

Single Sided 6/6
(plus packing and postage 1/-)
Abdication Speech—*H.M. King Edward VIII*

BADGES, PINS AND BROOCHES
British Union Flash and Circle
Chromium Badge (Pin, Brooch or
Stud 1/-
British Union Flash and Circle
Chromium Tiepin (large) .. 9d.
British Union 3-colour Flash and
Circle Enamelled Tie Pin .. 1/-
British Union 3-colour Flash and
Circle Enamelled Brooch.. .. 1/-
British Union 3-colour Sup-
porters Badge .. .. 6d.
British Union Flash and Circle
Diamante Clip or Brooch .. 3/-
British Union Flash and Circle
Marcasite Clip or Brooch .. 5/-

PHOTOGRAPHS
The Leader, Size 12 x 10 Mounted
(4 different Studies) 2/6
The Leader 1/1 Plate.. .. .. 1/-
The Leader 8 x 6 (Mounted) .. 1/3
Leading British Union Person-
alities, Postcard .. .. .. 3d.
British Union Activities, Large
Selection (8½ x 6½) 1/-

PROPAGANDA SUNDRIES
British Union Song Sheets
12 Songs .. .. **1d.**
Propaganda Postcards Packets of 12 **6d.**
3-colour Circle and Flash pencils
2d. each or per dozen **1/9**
Circle and Flash Car Labels
(booklet of 50) .. .. **9d.**
British Union Slogans—Gummed
Backs—18 wordings with Union
Flag and British Union Standard
in 3-colour 10 x 2½ ins. 2d. per
doz. or per 100 .. .. **1/4**

GENERAL SUNDRIES
Tumblers, Glass. Sand blast
Circle and Flash .. .. .. **4d.**
Ash Trays, Glass. 3-colour
Circle and Flash **1/3**
Memo Mirrors, with slogan and
Circle and Flash .. .. .. **4d.**
Cuff-Links, 3-colour Circle and
Flash. Good quality **2/-**
Rings, Signet, gold-plated with
2-colour Circle and Flash .. **2/-**
Cravats, Red Silk with 3-colour
Circle and Flash emblem .. **2/-**
Ties, Black with Gold flash .. **2/-**
Chromium Table Stands, with
3-colour bannerette **2/6**
Plaques of the Leader, Plaster
Cast, Bronze—
Hand finished **3/6**
Machine Finished **2/-**
Action and Blackshirt Binders each **3/6**
"Action" subscription rates—
Three months **3/3**
Six months **6/6**
Twelve months.. .. .. **13/-**
"Blackshirt" subscription rates—
Twelve months.. .. .. **1/6**
(All three editions) Twelve months **4/-**
"British Union Quarterly"—
Twelve months.. .. .. **4/6**
Calenders—1939—with photo of
Leader .. .. **6d.**
British Union Diaries 1939 .. **1/-**
,, ,, ,, with wallet **2/6**
Zinc Stencils—Leader's Head
with slogan **2/6**
Circle and Flash Notepaper, two
quires envelopes and paper .. **1/-**
Car and Cycle pennant—Circle
and Flash **1/4**

**For information and advice on
matters relating to books or litera-
ture write to the British Union
Bookshops, or Greater Britain Publications. We can get any book you
want.**
When ordering please include a little extra
to cover postage.

Published by the Greater Britain Publications (Abbey Supplies Ltd.), Sanctuary Bldgs., Grt.
Smith St., Westminster, S.W.1. ABBEY 1704 (6 lines)

Action, December 10th 1938.

B.U.F. election rosette.

Printed brassard as worn by stewards, late 1930's.

'The Blackshirt', 1935.

'Action', 1937.

'Action', 1937.

Action August 5th 1939

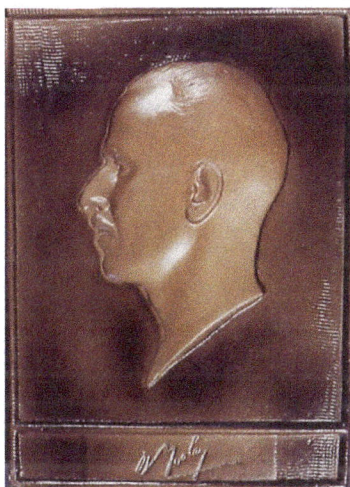

Machine finished plaque.

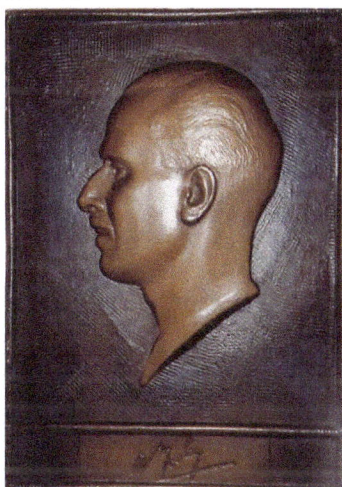

Hand finished plaque.

'Flash ties' for wear in civilian clothes.

ROYAL STAFFORD

BONE CHINA

MADE IN ENGLAND

"WE GIVE OURSELVES TO BRITAIN-
WE STAND FOR PEACE."

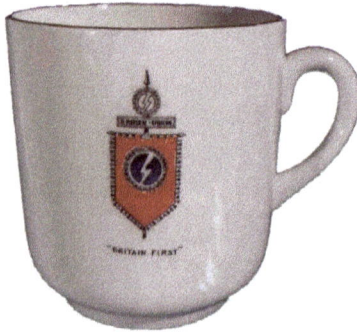

Royal Stafford cup bearing B.U.F. Honour Standard design.

Shield cuff links. 1935.

CUFF LINKS

NEW ISSUE   B.U.F. PATTERN

ENAMELLED WITH   **2/-** PER PAIR
FASCES & UNION JACK   POST FREE

SPECIAL DISCOUNT FOR QUAN- **Q.M. STORES**
TITIES. CASH WITH ORDER TO

Brooch, 1938.

SLEEVE LINKS

Silver and Black Enamel
Rhodium Plated ... 8/6

5

FOR THE LADIES

Brooch (as 8)
Paste Diamond ... 3s.
Marcasites ... 5s.
Plain Chromium ... 1s.

Post free, from.—

T. C. NOBBS,
53 Gorringe Park Avenue,
Mitcham, Surrey.
or British Union Bookshops

Action December 31st 1938.

Enamelled cuff links.

A FEW
BLACKSHIRT
AUTOMOBILE
C L U B
BADGES
For Disposal as Souvenirs

Chromium plated Circle and Flash crossed
with an embossed Fasces 3¼" in diameter

1/-

DISTRICTS 3 for 2/3,   12 for 9/-
Blackshirt Bookshop, Abbey Supplies Ltd

The Blckshirt Automobile Club badges were individually stamped on the reverse
with the owner's membership number. The above badge is numbered 46.

Swimming suit motif.

A fascist fork used at
Black House HQ, 1935.

BUF playing cards made by
De La Rue, 1935.

SPORTS
BELTS

WITH REPLICA OF
B.U. STANDARD

2/6 ea.

BRITISH UNION BOOKSHOPS

Sports belt buckle.

BUF Dairies for the years 1933,1939 and 1940.

Publicity stencil 'Mosley Will Win'
late 1930's.

Something New !
ZINC STENCIL of the LEADER'S HEAD

This Stencil is made of zinc, is 18" x 12" wide. Can be used for all kinds of outdoor publicity work, and will make very attractive posters. On the bottom of the Stencil are the words **MOSLEY WILL WIN.**

Price 2/6 from
ABBEY SUPPLIES LTD.
GREAT SMITH STREET
WESTMINSTER

The Blackshirt 6th March, 1937.

Canadian Union of Fascists
and Overseas Branches

During the early 1930's branches of the B.U.F. were formed by supporters living in many countries. Branches flourished not only in such European cities as Berlin, Paris and Rome (the first B.U.F. branch to be formed overseas was in Milan during April 1933), but also in Latvia, The West Indies, Singapore and Hong Kong. One such organisation was the Canadian Union of Fascists (later shortened to Canadian Union). The C.U.F. was formed in Winnipeg in 1934 as a Canadian Branch of the B.U.F. However, although remaining affiliated to the Mosley Movement, it soon developed into an independent organisation with an identity of its own. The C.U.F. adopted the black shirt as its uniform and used an emblem which incorporated the Canadian National symbol. Their emblem was designed by a Lutheran minister the Rev. Kaspereit and consisted of a triangle with a maple leaf in the centre crossed by a lightning flash (or thunderbolt)[53] .

B.U.F. Chief of Staff Ian Hope Dundas opens the Milan branch, 1933.

---

53 *The History of the Thunderbolt.* Dr. Fields.

18B Internment Camp, Ascot, Surrey. 1942.

The front and back covers of a detainees autograph book.

Internment Under Regulation 18B

In May 1940 Mosley was arrested and detained without charge or trail under Defence Regulation 18B. Over the next few weeks 800 members of the B.U.F. were to follow him into prison under this infamous act. It was claimed by opponents that this action was to frustrate possible fifth column activity by Mosley's supporters. However, many members of the B.U.F. fought and died for their country in this unnecessary war.

B.U.F. Political prisoners languish in internment Isle of Man, 1941

Items worn by former 18b detainees, and a Canteen voucher from the Peveril Interment Camp, Isle of Man. c.1941.

Union Movements first march, May 1948.

National European banner produced in the 1960's for use with the
Honour Standard.

Union Movement 1948 – 1975

After Mosley's wartime internment along with over 800 of his followers, he resumed his political activities in February 1948, with the formation of a new organisation 'Union Movement'. The U.M. advocated the political, economic, and cultural union of all Europe. Mosley proposed to include our former Dominions, South Africa and part of South America to form a great 'third force' in the world, independent of both capitalist America and the communist bloc.

Mosley was the first politician to recognize the problems of coloured immigration in the early 1950's, and the U.M. campaigned throughout its existence for a programme of repatriation. This promised that the immigrants would be returned to good jobs and homes in their countries of origin. The 'Union Movement' never hid the fact that it was a direct continuation of the B.U.F. The pre-war emblem of a Flash and Circle was retained, and the flags, drums and other trappings of the pre-war Movement were proudly used.

In 1962 in an effort to form a Europe-wide political force, Mosley's Union Movement joined with like minded European Movements to form an umbrella organisation, 'The National Party of Europe'. At a conference in Venice it was decided that they would strive for 'Europe a Nation' which meant that Europe would have a common government for purposes of foreign policy, defence, economic policy, finance and scientific development. The 'European Declaration of Venice', as the agreement was called, was signed by representatives from Italy's M.S.I., the German Deutsche Reichspartei and the Belgium M.A.C.

To complete the story of the B.U.F. and its regalia, I have briefly covered on the following pages some aspects, which U.M. inherited from its much larger predecessor.

Union Movement flags at a meeting in Shoreditch, July 1951.

Union Movement Flags

As stated earlier in the text the pre-war Honour Standards were used minus the BRITISH UNION box by the U.M. The B.U.F. Flash and Circle flags were also still used, very few professionally made new flags seem to have been acquired. Exceptions to this were a number of branch flags produced in the 1950's and 1960's. These oblong flags were made of black cotton and bore a central Flash and Circle in yellow, the branch's name appeared in large letters below the emblem, although there were variations to this style.

Another new flag which appeared in the early 1950's and would seem to have been a one off, consisted of an oblong red field on which was a central design of a white flash passing through a black roundel. The U.M. newspaper *Union* actually advertised armbands featuring this design in 1952. A U.M. veteran has stated that this was the flag of the 'Mosley Youth'

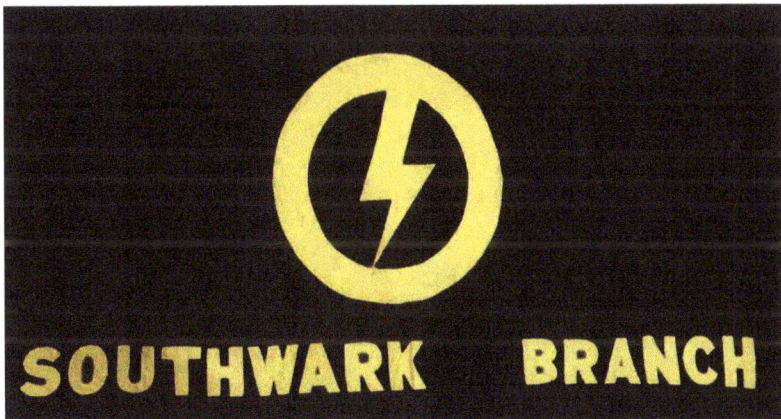

Union Movement branch flag c.1960.

Oswald Mosley speaks at Trafalgar Square, London. July 13th 1962.

Oswald Mosley greeted by supporters at Ridley Road, Dalston. May 1950.

Union Movement Award Badges

Following the pre-war practice the U.M. introduced a number of special award badges, for members who had excelled themselves in service to the Movement. The first post-war special award badge was officially described as 'The Leader's Special Award Badge Jan 1951-Dec 1953', It was awarded to members who had carried on active work during this period, or had been victimised or suffered in an extreme manner for their political activities. The badge was awarded to 95 U.M. members. No certificate was awarded with the badge, although members unable to attend the 1954 Annual Conference to receive the badge personally from the Leader of U.M. were sent the badge with a personal letter of thanks signed by Sir Oswald Mosley.

The bronze metal badge was in the form of a cut out Flash and Circle and had a red enamel bar at the base, on which was inscribed FOR SUSTAINED SERVICE 1951-1953.

In 1955 an Election Award Badge was presented to members who '… by their service in East London and Brixton before and during the L.C.C.Election campaign, gave such service on street work that it is considered worthy of recognition'. The badge was awarded to 64, mostly London members, for their work in this particularly successful campaign. Like the earlier award badge, Mosley presented members with the badge during the Annual Conference. The small silver coloured badge was again in the form of a cut out Flash and Circle and had a light blue enamel bar at its base on which was inscribed MARCH 1955.

THE LEADER'S ERAR'S

SPECIAL AWARD BADGE

Included in the list of members who
have qualified, are the undermentioned

Anderson.S.	Manchester	Irvine.S.L.	St.Osyth
Atherton.S.	Manchester	Irvine.Mrs.L.	St.Osyth
Aitken.B.	Putney	Jones.H.O.	Shoreditch
Bailey.F.	Bethnal Green	Kirk.M.	Finsbury park
Bailey.J.	Bethnal Green	Kerby.L.	Islington
Bailey.S.	Bethnal Green	Kitchen.K.	Lincoln
Beard.A.R.	Hackney	Ince s.H.	Kilburn
Beard.Wm.	Shoreditch	McKevitt.Mrs.M.	Welworth
Beard.Miss.K.	Shoreditch	McKevitt.R.	Welworth
Brown.C.	Salford	Martin.Miss D.	Highbury
Brodey.J.	Woodford	Mendham.F.	Clapton
Burton.L.	Shrewsbury	McDonald.J.	Prestwich
Burton.Mr..R.	Shrewsbury	Marsh.Miss M.	St.John's Wood
Beecroft.H.	Gt.Yarmouth	Main.Miss C.M.	Perthshire
Capleton.L.	Bristol	Nicols.J.V.J.	Dagenham
Bright.R.	Harrow	Nash.Miss V.	Shoreditch
Cudden.A.M.	Southall	Orrin.Miss E.	Marylebone
Clayden.P.	Ipswich	Price-Heywood.F.B.	Grasmere
Coyle.P.	Enfield	Prentice.C.	Forest gate
Cork.F.R.	Kings Lynn	Prentice.Mrs.R.	Forest gate
Clayton.C.	Finsbury	Phelan.F.E.	Sheffield
Crisp.R.	South Woodford	Pegg.R.	Holloway
Churnley.J.Wm.	Southport	Price.C.	Homerton
Clark.R.N.	Worcester	Price.L.	Homerton
Dunig.P.P.	Millwall	Quill.M.	Stoke Newington
Dods.W.	Hampstead	Rou.R.	Lancaster
Draper.H.	Portsmouth	Rourke.G.	Manchester
Derby.Mrs.F.	Finsbury Park	Rose.Miss E.	Forest Gate
Dawson.Miss L.	Cardiff	Rose.Miss M.	Forest Gate
Elliott.C.W.	Boscombe East	Roberts.Miss W.	Taunton
Elliott.Mrs.R.	Boscombe East	Rowlands.J.	Liverpool
English.R.M.	Chingford	Sutherland.Mrs.M.A.	Limehouse
Eaton.H.	Stepney	Saunders.R.	Dorchester
Evans.E.C.	East Dulwich	Sweetland.R.	Camden Town
Franklin.A.L.	Kilburn	Scott.A.	Nottingham
Fields.W.	Shoreditch	Smith.J.	Bermondsey
Franklin.R.	Enfield	Sreeten.G.	Walthamstow
Firth.E.H.	West Hartlepool	Sandercock.G.	Dover
Goodwin.P.	Isle of Wight	Thatcher.J.	Salisbury
Gibson.T.	Finsbury	Troke.R.	Marylebone
Gibson.K.	Crayford	Tidy.C.T.	Islington
Haydey.Miss F.	Bethnal Green	Traynor.F.	Forest Hill
Haydey.Miss R.	Bethnal Green	Titcombe.A.	Aylesbury
Humpneys.H.	Mitcham	Vine.F.	Ladbroke Grove
Horsley.L.B.	Leeds	White.F.	Bethnal Green
Hamley.F.	Sheffield	Warburton.J.	Battersea
Holliwell.J.	Hackney	Webb.R.	Watford
	Williamson.J.G.	Edinburgh	

A list of U.M. members who qualified for the 1951-53 Award badge.

Further award badges were presented to members for electoral work at least up until the late 1960's. These would appear mostly to take the form of the earlier 1954 badge, being made of a bronze metal (although a similar badge in chrome is known) with a red enamel bar with the wording FOR SERVICE. This is not a complete listing of award badges and other designs may have been used.

UNION ⊘ **MOVEMENT**

LEADER : OSWALD MOSLEY.

302, VAUXHALL BRIDGE ROAD,
VICTORIA, LONDON, S.W. I
Telephone VICtoria 7466/7.

F. Hamley Esq.,
SHEFFIELD.   5th October 1954.

My Dear Hamley,

            This is to send to you the Badge of Honour
which it would have been my pride and pleasure to
present to you at the Annual Conference if you had
been able to be present.

            Thank you so much for all you have done.

                    Yours in Union,

Letter to U.M. member F. Hamley who was unable to attend the 1954 Conference.

Sir Oswald Mosley presents a Special Award Badge 1951–1953 at the Union Movement Annual Meeting 1954. The recipient is Fred Bailey the U.M. Organiser in Bethnal Green. Note the Honour Standard top still bearing the British Union box.

Oswald Mosley presents an Election Award Badge to Raven Thomson, at the 1955 Union Movement Annual Conference. Note the Mosley Youth flag in the background.

ELECTION AWARDS BADGES

During the Conference the Leader will present Election Award Badges to the undermentioned, who by their service in East London and or Brixton before and during the L.C.C. Election Campaign gave such service on "street" work that is considered worthy of recognition.

Aitken.B.	Putney	Irvine.S.L.	East Essex
Anderson.G.	Shoreditch	Joyce.S.	Stepney
Bailey.F.	Bethnal Green	Jones.H.	Shoreditch
Bailey.S.	" "	Jackson.J.	"
Bailey.Mrs.D.	" "	Kerby.L.	"
Beard.W.	Shoreditch	Kerby.Mrs.L.E.	"
Beard.Mrs.C.	"	Marsh.Miss M.	Nth.London
Borkwood.B.	N.H.Q.	Maughan.T.	Bethnal Green
Coates.A.V.	Morden	McKevitt.R.	Brixton
Cuddon.A.M.	Ealing	McKevitt.Mrs.M.	"
Cuddon.R.A.	"	Proud.S.	Shoreditch
Darby.Mrs.F.	Shoreditch	Preston.M.	Youth
Duhig.P.	Bethnal Green	Parsons.Miss	Nth.London
Duplock.W.	Stepney	Pacey.M.T.	Brixton
Dods.W.	Hampstead	Pacey.Mrs.P.	"
Eaton.H.	Shoreditch	Roythorne.C.	Tottenham
English.R.M.	Kensington	Row.R.	Brixton
Elliott.C.W.	Bournemouth	Ryan.M.J.	"
Elliott.Mrs.F.	"	Sutton.G.	"
Foster.J.	Shoreditch	Sutton.Mrs.P.	"
Fields.W.	"	Saunders.R.	Bournemouth
Fieldhouse.M.	"	Sutherland.Mrs.	Bethnal Green
Fraser.P.A.	Ealing	Sweetman.G.	Walthamstow
Evans.E.C.	N.H.Q.	Tidy.C.T.	Nth.London
Gibson.T.	Shoreditch	Thomson.A.R.	Kensington
Gibson.K.	Youth	Quill.M.	Hackney
Good.Miss A.	Bethnal Green	Warren.G.E.	Stepney
Gusterton.C.	Tottenham	Wade.J.	"
Hamm.E.J.	Nth.London		
Horwood.L.	Bethnal Green	----------------------------	
Hayday.Miss F.	" "		
Hayday.Miss R.	" "	E. M. S.............	
Holliwell.O.	" "		
Humphreys.J.	Brixton	Election Workers & Agents.	
Hudson.G.	"	See announcment back page.	
Hudson.Mrs.S.	"	----------------------------	

A full list of U.M. members who qualified for the 1955 Election Award badge.

Mosley speaks to a large crowd at Dalston, 1948.

Oswald Mosley speaks at Trafalgar Square, London. July 13th 1962.

U.M. Miscellaneous

Like the pre-war B.U.F., the Union Movement and its branches produced merchandise to raise funds. These included items like 'British Union style belts, pure leather with the Flash and Circle on the buckle', which sold at 25/- (£1-25). Other items included felt pennants and brassards, a selection of which are shown below.

CIRCLE and FLASH PENNANTS

Only 2s. IId. Each

Colours Red, White and Blue
Size 8″ × 18″.   Special price
for orders of 6 or more.
Wholesale prices for Bookshops
and Branches.
Packing and Postage 3d. extra.
SEND YOUR ORDERS NOW TO
EAST ESSEX BRANCH
BOX No. 249
302 Vauxhall Bridge Road,
Victoria, S.W.1.

'Union' May 10th 1952

147

Union Movement lapel badges produced between 1948 - 1975.

The man who never gave up. Denied access to most meeting halls, and a press and television boycott, Mosley was forced to speak at public venues. Here Mosley is speaking at a street meeting in Cheshire Street, Bethnal Green. September 1965.

www.ingramcontent.com/pod-product-compliance
Lightning Source LLC
Chambersburg PA
CBHW050805270326
41926CB00025B/4550